*Enjoy my Wrinkly Bits! Happy cruising! Gail Cushman September 2021*

Wrinkly Bits

# Cruise Time

A Wrinkly Bits Senior Hijinks Romance

Gail Decker Cushman

# Endorsements

"Cushman's writing in her *Wrinkly Bits* series is fresh, smart, and makes me look forward to a spicier second half of life. Here's to senior romance; it sounds a heck of a lot more fun than twenty-somethings on Tinder."

AK Turner,
*New York Times* bestselling author of
*This Little Piggy Went to the Liquor Store*

"*Cruise Time*, the first book in Gail Cushman's *Wrinkly Bits* series, kept me entertained as Audrey Lyon packs her bags—both literally and figuratively—and sets sail with her husband of nearly fifty years. Can they rekindle the spark, or will Audrey spend her time fantasizing about having an affair with a handsome stranger? I highly recommend this book!"

Laurie Buchanan,
author of *Note to Self, The Business of Being*,
and the Sean McPherson suspense/thriller novels.

"Gail Cushman's new book, *Cruise Time*, is a delightful comedy and reminds us that romance is not merely for the under 30s. It is both funny and poignant, and I can't wait to read the next volume of her series, *Wrinkly Bits*."

Patricia Werhane,
documentary producer,
BIG QUESTIONS PRODUCTIONS.

"Gail Cushman's *Wrinkly Bits* books are well-written and homey, with delightful tongue-in-cheek story telling. These books were a breath of fresh air."

Chuck Sacrison
Book Reviewer, LTC Retired, U.S. Army

"The refreshing whimsy in these pages is a welcomed perspective as I navigate the season of life where I can hardly fathom doing anything other than chasing around my four little kids and trying to keep up with the general chaos of life. Cushman's capacity for shaping a scene and an experience through words and wit are like a mini vacation—and, filled with heart and tenderness to spark reflection and proper prioritization in life."

**Megan Bryant,**
**Improv Trainer and Award-winning Comedian and Author**

"I've often wondered why there are so few books about senior romances. So I was delighted to happen upon Gail Cushman's *Wrinkly Bits* series. These books are clever reminders that much of life actually does begin after 60, when the kids are gone, money has been saved, and bucket lists need attention. I flew through the first two in the series, *Cruise Time* and *Out of Time*, during our last Mediterranean cruise!"

**Barbara Jo Charters**
**Ageless Adventurer and 53-time Cruiser**

"I absolutely love being in the midst of a book only to find myself smiling, chuckling, even pausing for the occasional chortle and good old fashioned belly laugh. Gail Cushman's humor shines through *Wrinkly Bits* sharing fun tales of travel through the eyes of adventurous seniors, and it proves to be just what you need to brighten your day. Looking forward to the next books in the series!"

**Cindy Turner,**
**Travel Advisor**

"There should be more books out there like this! There is so much of life to be lived and Gail Cushman's *Wrinkly Bits* series made me laugh and think there is so much adventure ahead in our lives, we just have to be willing. Cushman's books are easy to read and highly entertaining."

Lori Hosac,
Sales Manager

"Since retiring I have had more time to read and have looked forward to Gail Cushman's blog *Wrinkly Bits*. So I was happy to learn of her series of books with the same title. Their light-hearted nature is especially welcome during the challenging times we all are experiencing now."

Jim Mitchell
Owner Jim's IGA, Mitchell's IGA,
and D9 IGA in Idaho.

Edited by AnnaMarie McHargue and Anita Stephens
Designed by Leslie Hertling

www.wrinklybits.com

*Dedicated to*
*Thomas Cushman, RIP*
*Lover, Husband, and Cruisemate*

# CHAPTER 1
## Audrey

*My name is Audrey Lyon, and I'm going on a cruise. It's my first one ever. I don't know where I'm going, because my husband of nearly fifty years just walked through the door and told me to dig out the old suitcases, and while I am at it, toss in a bikini.*

"Time to get ready, Hon, we're going on a cruise," Griff shouted, as he stormed through the screened back door. Griff, returning from an annual reunion with his Navy buddies, had always insisted he didn't take pleasure in cruises, even though he had never been on one except for the time he had floated the Gulf of Tonkin during the Vietnam conflict. He preferred to spend his free time with a fishing pole or rifle in hand, depending on the season. Hunting season fell in the fall and fishing season covered the other nine months. I don't do either.

"Cruise? Where are we going? A bikini? I am nearly seventy years old!" I asked incredulously. "When?"

"Portugal or Spain, or maybe France. It doesn't matter. Wherever the damn boat goes. Gus and Steve and their wives are going, and I decided we should go with them. We need to be in Fort Lauderdale Sunday night, to *embark*, they call it, on Monday afternoon. I have the tickets for the cruise, but we need to fly to Fort Lauderdale, and I don't have those tickets yet. Isn't your friend Cindy a travel agent? Call her and get the tickets."

*Oh, great! We're going someplace, we just don't know where.*

"Wait a minute, Griff, who are Gus and Steve, and why did you decide to go on this cruise? You hate cruises, you've always said so. Remember three years ago, when I tried to surprise you with a Caribbean cruise for our fiftieth? I got our passports and all the documents and saved money to pay for it, but when the kids blabbed about it, you put the kibosh on it, saying you'd had enough cruise time in the Gulf of Tonkin. Remember we ended up fishing at the Redhorn Lodge because they had stocked the lake that week?" *I recalled that trip being a four-book, two-bottles of wine weekend.*

"I might have been wrong about the Caribbean trip, but I want to do this," he argued.

*He hasn't admitted he was wrong since Nixon was impeached. What's going on here?*

"Did you say we have to be in Fort Lauderdale Sunday? You mean tomorrow night? And the ship leaves on Monday? And you don't know for sure where we are traveling?" I skeptically asked, panicked at his sudden desire to travel on a boat.

*I'd been to Navy reunions before and found them God-awful, with former sailors bragging about their fleet feats, most of which were untrue. As bored as I was in Hunter, I hadn't had the strength to weather another discussion of their bogus activities. As it turned out, I should have gone, in order to lobby for going to France, my life's dream.*

*So, we have tickets someplace, but he doesn't know where. We have to be in Florida tomorrow, and I don't have anything new to wear or read. He wants to spend time with his Navy pals, who will be boring and probably as rude as he has become since he retired. Wow. Sounds like a real barrel of monkeys.*

Griff interrupted my cynical thoughts. "Yes, the ship departs on Monday at 4 o'clock, but they told me we can get on the ship earlier than that. It's a repositioning cruise, so I guess that's why it was cheaper than a regular cruise. It's a new line named *The Broadsomething*. The guys told me they had reservations at the Ritzy-Que near the piers, and we could grab an Uber to the ship, whatever an Uber is. We've seen the Ritzy-Que ads on TV."

*Of course, it will be cheap, that's not new.*

I shook my head, "We've never used an Uber. Do you know how much it will cost or how you do it? I haven't heard of the Ritzy-Que before, and it sounds expensive, too. I'll have Cindy find us a less expensive one."

"No. To hell with the cost. For once in our lives, let's be impulsive, spontaneous. Everybody uses Ubers, and I've heard they cost less than taxies. You can look in the phone book for Uber's phone number. It must be easy," Griff scowled at me, not considering I might have an opinion.

*A telephone book? Do they even still publish those? We haven't had one in the last decade.*

"To hell with the cost? You've never said that before. You worry about the cost of everything," I objected, wondering if he had injured his head. "You know, Griff, spontaneity is not in your bailiwick. What happened at your reunion to make you Mr. Do-It-Now? And, who are Gus and Steve?"

He protested, "I'm spontaneous, what do you mean? Just yesterday, at the reunion, I bought the cruise tickets, just did it, no foreplay. But I'll show you spontaneous."

He walked over, grabbed me around the waist, and laid a juicy one on my lips, "I love you, Hon." He let go of me and poured himself a giant cup of coffee and added cream. "Third cup of coffee today. With cream and a hug and a smooch for my girl. Look at me! Mr. Spontaneous." He proceeded through the door aiming toward the barn, leaving me, as always, alone in the kitchen.

*What the heck is happening? And, for Pete's sake, a bikini?*

# CHAPTER 2
## *Audrey*

Griff and I married a few days before he shipped out to Vietnam with the Navy fleet, spending his thirteen-month tour aboard the aircraft carrier, *Iwo Jima*. Except for the trip to Hawaii for R & R midway through his tour, we had not left the states. While in Honolulu, we watched Don Ho's night club show, got to hear him play his signature song *Tiny Bubbles*, and dined at a romantic restaurant or two. But Griff had craved McDonald's fries, so we gravitated to the golden arches more than a few times. We also visited the Dole plantation and went to the USS Arizona monument, followed by a premiere viewing of *Tora, Tora, Tora*, which was sobering, to say the least. With so much activity, I don't know how I managed to get pregnant on that trip.

After his tour overseas ended, we settled down in Hunter, Idaho, a little community of fewer than 35,000 people, where Griff farmed hops and soybeans. Any activity beyond planting and harvesting, in his mind, was a waste of time. So mainly, we just waited for each season to come and go. It was about as exciting as watching mudholes fill with water on a rainy day.

I never much liked Hunter, which lay in the heart of Idaho farm country where onions, sugar beets, soybeans, and, of course, Idaho potatoes grew. In hindsight, I would have preferred the big city, but here I am, stuck in the same place for fifty years doing little more than watching things grow: hops for beer, grapes for wine, and potatoes for vodka.

*Now as I think about it, all of the alcoholic beverages being grown and available at my fingertips should have led to a vibrant social life, but somehow, we never got around to it.*

Griff was a homebody and preferred spending time under the open sky rather than under a roof. Farming had suited him, and he excelled at it. I thought him an enigma because he had an opinion on everything but didn't articulate well. Before he retired, he liked to converse with the cows, but afterwards opted for hunting for Bambi or pulling in Nemo. Seldom me.

I, on the other hand, was the family's social secretary, flitting from chicken to chicken because of the scarcity of social gatherings. After college, I worked part-time as an LPN in a chemical dependency center, doing absolutely nothing with my French, a degree I had worked my tail off to earn. I drove the twenty miles out of Hunter three days a week, using my driving time to reconcile my frustrations and loneliness.

We raised two sons, Jeff and Mike, and did everything by the book, but cheaply. I milked the cows and gathered the eggs to reduce our grocery bills, but when we sold the farm, all the animals went away. I wished we had sold the house and barn, too, maybe move downtown where there were more things to do, but Griff always told me we'd grow old here. So now, without even a chicken to keep me company, I have even less to do.

*I had been reduced to talking to soybeans, and now Griff's offer has shaken me like an earthquake. I don't know how to react, or what to think.*

# CHAPTER 3
## *Audrey*

I called my friend Cindy fearing no seats would be available to Lauderdale at this late date, but she found us two first-class tickets on the flight from Salt Lake. The extra costs for the upgrade made little difference to me, but I knew Griff would blow a gasket. He'd just have to live with it if we had any chance of getting to Florida on time. We'd have to change planes twice after leaving the Boise airport, once in Salt Lake City and once in Atlanta, but would arrive in Lauderdale before dark.

I thought about carrying a mini bottle of whiskey, or maybe more, on the flight in case Griff became contrary, or I got fed up with his sometimes pigheaded behavior, but Cindy assured me the first-class section would take good care of us.

My next calls were to the boys to let them know of the spur-of-the-moment trip. They both laughed and said something snarky, suggesting their dad had lost his mind.

*Memo to self: Check Griff's head for gashes or other injuries.*

Our retirement didn't change who we were, but rather how we dealt with our new routines. Griff had always worked alone but was not lonely. He worked hard at fishing and hunting, conversing with nature, and threw lovemaking in for spice. The four provided a winning hand.

*Maybe that's all HE needed, but I didn't fish, and I didn't hunt, and with Griff's third avocation, my lower forty got more workouts than rocking chairs in a room full of cats.*

On the other hand, I was more amicable than Griff and relished the flurry of nursing in the treatment center downtown, and although I had only worked part-time, I now missed seeing and hearing from my co-workers and friends.

In the beginning, I wondered what my coworkers might be doing on this day or that, but soon I settled into my own version of *Groundhog Day*, with every day the same. My friends in town who were similarly retired became involved in their own activities. A few played cards or mahjong, others volunteered in non-profits. I, on the other hand, listened to the tick of my grandfather clock watching the hops and soybeans grow and flies buzz around on the bedroom ceiling.

I tried, I really did, to alleviate my discontent. I read voraciously, plowing through the free Kindle books, listening to books while walking my 10,000 steps through the pastures every day. I knitted a scarf, but I forgot to count the rows and soon it was fourteen feet long, so I abandoned that project. I joined a book club, but they only met once a month. Church filled parts of Sundays, but Griff didn't want to go, and people asked me why, so I stopped churchgoing to avoid the interrogations. I liked to cook, but I was tired of my old recipes, and Griff refused to eat new ones. Television didn't interest me, and Griff's favorite channel, the sex channel, led to his pleasure and my fatigue.

*I approached retirement loving food and coffee, but only six months in I feared becoming a hungry alcoholic.*

I had longed to travel, to see the world, to recapture and use my lost and lagging French language skills, but Griff preferred staying home, never needing or wanting to branch out. I had imagined practicing my French in foreign lands, but over the years instead spoke my second language only to the chickens. Speaking French to the soybeans, I found, was too pathetic.

Griff's notion of taking a cruise caught me by surprise and since I didn't know the itinerary, I packed in a hurry, throwing in swimsuits, but not a bikini, and last summer's shorts, crossing my fingers they still fit. But I immediately took them out, replacing them with long pants and sweaters that I knew fit. But then, for good luck, tossed in a few pairs of shorts after all, some a size larger, in case we had warm weather, something I certainly would welcome after another tedious winter in Hunter. Surely the cruise ship will have a store.

We needed to rise before dawn to catch our flight, and as I closed the suitcases, I knew something was missing. A book or two to fall back on if I became bored on the cruise. I fingered three, wondering which to bring. I had read them all. One choice was *Gone with the Wind* because it featured all the checkmarks: romantic, historical, and long. Especially long. Choice two was *The Catcher in the Rye*. If Griff didn't enjoy the cruise, I might become as depressed as Holden Caulfield and develop simpatico with him. Choice three was *The Graduate*, so I could fantasize about having an affair with a handsome and far younger man. Here's to you, Mr. Robinson. Ha. As if.

## CHAPTER 4
### *Audrey*

After an uneventful day of travel, the Fort Lauderdale Ritzy-Que expected Griff and me and provided red-carpet treatment as a bellhop ushered us to our room on the sixth floor. The vintage hotel was in a state of repair, but thankfully the elevator worked, at least to our floor, as it creaked and sputtered when we entered. It had thirty or more floors with a large lobby, but our assigned room was undoubtedly the tiniest hotel room I had ever stayed in. The room, shaped in an "L," had the bed snuggled tightly into the vertical, so we would have to crawl over the bed to sleep. The puffy white coverlet was a plus, and a miniature settee gave us room to sit. One at a time. Although frayed and faded, it would do for one night. A tiny balcony faced another high-rise hotel and contained two small patio chairs and a small glass table. Its black wrought-iron fence offered barely enough maneuvering room to stand and scan the neighborhood. "What a lovely balcony," I voiced to the bellman, trying to be positive. I looked around but didn't see a bathroom, "Where is the bathroom?" I asked, growing concerned.

"Down the hall, three doors on the right. Be sure to take the sign with you. As you can tell, we are in renovation mode and bathrooms are being added to every room, so next time you stay with us, you will have a genuinely nice bath." He pointed to a sign on the wall *Pardon Our Progress* and handed me a laminated *Do Not Disturb* sign while holding his hand out for a tip. Griff looked at me with dismay but laid a picture of Jackson in the bellman's hand. This was definitely not the Griff I know.

The bellman left, and Griff said, "Let's go to the bar, I could use a drink." He nudged me toward the door. "I'm as thirsty as a dusty soybean field."

"You go ahead, I want to switch into shorts and try out the DND sign. I hope it works. I'll be down in a few minutes," I answered, resisting his nudge.

Griff left the room, saying, "Don't be long. You know I don't like to be kept waiting."

"There are so many things you don't enjoy," I mumbled quietly to myself as I picked up the DND sign and went down the hall.

Griff, dressed in his characteristic jeans, green plaid shirt, and black tennis shoes, entered the hotel bar, already filled with guests who were dressed in brightly colored cruise clothes. The guests sat at the small round tables scattered throughout the room sipping on pink, blue, and amber drinks, munching on peanuts with only two tables remaining vacant. A gentle murmur of conversation rippled through the darkened room, and Griff scanned the crowd several times before his eyes landed on a table where two men sat with drinks and a plate of nachos. "Griff, you decided to come with us. Great! What made you change your mind? Come sit down with us. Did your wife come with you?"

"Yes, she did. She's taking care of business and will come down in a few minutes. She's a little irked that we don't have a bathroom in our room. I'm just wondering, do your rooms have baths or do you have to *go down the hall*, too? I haven't seen a room without a bathroom since we were in the Navy, half a century ago."

Steve agreed, "I know, Phyllis and Carlee aren't happy either, but it's just one night. The good thing is that this hotel lies close to the pier, walking distance, if we didn't have all our luggage. It's gonna be a great trip though." The three men began rearranging their chairs, squeezing two more around the table, making room for six.

## CHAPTER 5
### *Audrey*

Even though I knew Griff was waiting, I wanted to take my time, so I walked down the six flights of stairs to the ground floor where I assumed that I would find Griff. The front desk was centered in the large lobby, but I saw nothing resembling a bar. I moved from here to there, and back again, looking for a bar where Griff no doubt would be drinking something. A distinguished-looking white-haired African American gentleman stopped me and asked, "Are you lost, Miss? May I help you?"

*Miss?* No one had called me *Miss* for a long time. After all, I am over sixty-five. I found myself flooded with insecurities and a flurry of questions. I glanced his way and moved my eyes to the nearby floor to ceiling mirror, wondering if he was talking to me, but there was no one else in the vicinity. I wondered if men could find me attractive with the innumerable sags and bags I mostly keep hidden, although I do try to stay in shape. My driver's license claimed my height at five-foot-six, but that was a lie since I had shrunk two full inches after retirement. My normally ginger hair was now streaked with gray, but my hairdresser, who might also have been a liar, advised me that many people would pay extra for silver highlights, so I didn't touch them up. I knew I couldn't pass for forty but didn't look eighty either. I wondered if my front half was still perky, and if my back half was taut enough to turn men's heads if I wore the right clothes. Was he talking to me? Why are my hands shaking?

"Miss," I heard again, "Are you lost?"

"No, I mean, yes, maybe. I'm trying to find the barn, I mean bar. I'm looking for a husband, I mean my husband. I mean, I don't drink, except wine, which doesn't count, but the other guy, I mean Griff, he drinks sometimes." Nothing coming out of my mouth was even remotely related to the truth, but the truth seemed to be the road less traveled.

I couldn't express a coherent sentence. Why was I babbling? And what about the sensations, tingling, throbbing, I was feeling in my lower forty? I felt as jumpy as a frog eyeing a frying pan. This man was alluring, almost mesmerizing. Every part of him from his eyes to his toes spoke to me, and I swept my eyes over him from top to bottom, twice, bewildered at not being able to speak without stammering. I had read about love at first sight but had never felt anything close since I fell for Griff.

"I'm Audrey Ryan, I mean Lyon, from Idaho, and I'm going on a boat, I mean a cruise." Not only couldn't I remember Griff's name, I couldn't remember mine. "I apologize for chattering. I don't know what's wrong with me because I don't usually do that." My face flashed red and hot, and strangely enough, I felt both rattled and free, like my body had jerked into overdrive leaving a cloud of dust behind. I was not myself, and for the time being, at least, I didn't know who I was. And didn't care.

The man shortened the distance between us and nestled my now-clammy hand in both of his. I tried to pull away, but he didn't let go. "No harm, no foul, as Alex Trebek likes to say. I'm Logan Hall from Oregon. I don't mean to be forward, but I noticed you walking in circles and thought you might be lost. The bar can be found on the other side of the lobby, so walk past the front desk and turn left after the fish tank. You'll locate it easily enough. And probably find a husband or your husband there, whichever you want." His charming smile enhanced the tingles to twitches, and my mind lay centered between a nerf-ball and a marshmallow.

I glanced down at my sweaty hand, which he still held, this time yanking it away and wiping it dry it on my shorts. I looked to where he pointed, thanked him, and beelined myself toward the fish tank before glancing back. He stood there, watching me, so I tossed a little wave and tried to say *thank you*, but it came out *Mazel Tov*. I had no idea why.

# CHAPTER 6
*Logan*

D r. Logan Hall originally hailed from Dade City, Florida, but life had taken him to Oregon after graduating *summa cum laude* from the University of Florida medical school, where he specialized in podiatry, and in particular, foot disorders. He wanted to work in a small town, but racism in Florida in the mid-1960s had closed some doors and slammed shut others. Physician or not, it became clear that his ability to practice his chosen profession in Dade City or other small southern towns ranged from dismal to not-gonna-happen. As a part of his internships, he volunteered his medical expertise to a group of climbers who scaled Mount St. Helens, pre-eruption, because serious climbers needed the services of podiatrists and orthopedic surgeons on their mountain treks. He fell in love with the Pacific Northwest and began searching for a community not only where he would be accepted, but with enough feet to make a good life for himself. Central Oregon won.

At seventy, Logan Hall was a fine-looking man who knew plenty of women aching to spend time with him. He had been the first African American doctor in Portland, Oregon, a mostly white, but racially tolerant, city. He and his wife had traveled extensively, and he had worked for Doctors Without Borders in Guatemala for over ten years. His wife, a Caucasian woman and a pediatrician, had wrestled with diabetes her entire adult life until finally succumbing four years ago.

On the taller side, Logan maintained his BMI at an optimal level. He was prone to vegetarianism, and seldom ate the white stuff, like sugar or flour. He paid attention to his general health with his 10,000 steps-a-day health plan, starting every morning with a two-mile walk, followed by another two miles after dinner. His midday walks rocketed his mileage to 12,000 steps or more.

Logan, smart and stylish, tuned into the latest fashions, head to foot—especially foot—and became a shoe aficionado owning more than a hundred pairs of sneakers, sandals, brogues, and boots. Oregon's Imelda Marcos, he liked to joke to himself. Quiet and unpretentious, he was indeed tall, dark, and handsome, but his friends declared that he was as plain as an old slipper.

He developed a good podiatry practice, married a lovely Caucasian wife, created good community relationships, and longed for nothing, absolutely nothing. But now, Joan was gone, dead for four years, and loneliness had set in. People cited his name first on Oregon's short list of worthy widowers, but most of his suitors searched either for money or status, and he had no interest in either bankrolling them or elevating them in the eyes of the community. He had earned a good life with plenty of money and status, and was an attractive prey for any cougar, but he missed Joan and tuned his pursuers out. A few women had approached him directly offering sexual favors and a happy lifestyle, but he experienced no chemistry and ignored them.

He and Joan had twin daughters, both married, Jan to Grant, and Laura Lee to Monique. Neither had kids, nor seemed in any hurry to procreate, although all four were in their late thirties. Both girls had moved to the east coast before Joan died, and they didn't visit Oregon often, citing its dullness. They never even added another adjective. Oregon was dull, dull, and dull.

After Joan had been gone two years, Logan retired and spent a year touring the United States with the goal of seeing every state capital. He bought a new Lexus and mapped out a route with only a few repeats, but after visiting thirty-eight capitals, the last being Tallahassee, Florida, he found being alone in the car for over a year intensified his loneliness and made him grow hungry for companionship. He knew he didn't necessarily want a permanent relationship but would enjoy companionship occasionally to share a movie or a glass of wine. He decided to terminate his tour temporarily and drove four hundred miles south to Fort Lauderdale, ready to try a new avocation. Cruising gave him the advantages of not having to unpack every day and included food and entertainment at a reasonable price. He rented a small Fort Lauderdale condo to serve as his home base and began his new cruising adventures.

His initial attraction to Audrey was sexual, no doubt about it. His pony turned stallion the first time she spoke, and he knew he was smitten. *No, I mean, yes, I mean maybe. I'm trying to find the barn, I mean bar. I'm looking for a husband, I mean my husband.* She had blushed beet red, and it lit his fire. A blush? A hot flash? It didn't matter since he had become instantly infatuated with how she looked, talked, and her nonplussed demeanor. She seemed giddy about something, could it be him?

A myriad of women of all ages, races, and backgrounds had tried to entice, involve, and seduce him since Joan died, but he had refused them all, ignoring their advances, willing them to leave him alone. It had been over four years since he had enjoyed an erection, but here he stood, in the middle of a hotel lobby, growing bigger and prouder with each word she spoke. Who was she, and why was he attracted to her?

## CHAPTER 7
*Audrey*

In the darkness of the bar, I managed to locate Griff and wove through the tables and chairs toward him. My skin was aflame, and I wondered about my female clamminess. I was perplexed at how a stranger could have affected me in such a manner since I had jumbled my sentences and words into unintelligible thoughts, as when I told him my name was Audrey Ryan instead of Lyon. *Mazel Tov? Really?* I ignored my naughty sensations and focused on removing the white-haired gentleman from my mind, but in trying delete him, I found myself fixated on him.

The two other men stood as I approached, and Griff bumped a chair in my direction with his foot. "This is my first wife, Audrey," he joked, wrapping his arm across my shoulders. His old joke ran stale, but he guffawed at it. The other two greeted me with, "My pleasure, I'm glad you decided to come," and "So glad you could join us," but I wasn't sure who said what because I was preoccupied with thoughts of the man in the lobby. These two friends of Griff seemed polite enough, certainly more polite than Griff had been recently. It seemed all Griff cared about was "doing the dirty," and he thought more was better. The blue pill was his pleasure but my nightmare.

"This is Steve Sanderson, and I'm Rich Gustafson, but everybody calls me Gus. We ran into Griff earlier this week at the Navy reunion."

Gus, a big boy probably several digits over his recommended BMI, showed bulging biceps despite the excess pounds. He wore black plaid shorts, a striped t-shirt with a Nike logo, and white compression socks with black tennis shoes. His protruding muscles strained the sleeves of his t-shirt. He reminded me of high school football referees: *zebras,* Griff called them. Gray and slightly bald, he compensated with a comb-over that swaddled most of his head. A footed cane sat next to his chair, but he subtly knocked it to the ground as I approached the table.

Gus wrapped his hand around a glass with something amber in it, maybe Scotch, maybe whiskey, but not beer. "I live in Hunter, same as you two, and I have a wife around here, but I'm not sure where. I was a teacher and probably had your kids in my physical education classes." He twisted his neck around, but not seeing her, returned his eyes to me, "I'm sure she'll be here soon."

The other man introduced himself, "I'm Steve Sanderson. My wife, Carlee, and I recently moved to Hunter from Salt Lake City. She wanted to be closer to our kids, and I wanted to get out of the big city squirrel cage. You'll meet her later. She wasn't feeling great this morning." Steve, with his bright yellow shorts and a tucked-in yellow and white striped polo shirt, appeared to be ready to board the ship. He weighed a little less than Griff and quite a few loaves of bread less than Gus. He had salt and pepper hair, a large, crooked nose, fair skin, and soft, uncalloused hands. He sat down again, crossed his legs, and placed his gray tweed flat cap on his knee. Two glasses sat in front of him, one empty and the other half full of dark red wine.

"Carlee's sick?" Griff asked. "She's going to go on the cruise, isn't she? She's the one who convinced me to come. She's tons of fun, and it wouldn't be the same without her."

Steve reached behind his ear to adjust his hearing aids and said, "Oh, hell, yeah, she'll be fine. She drank too much wine last night, and it caught up with her. She should be down in a few minutes."

I ordered a glass of Chardonnay, and Griff was drinking a craft beer he had never heard of before, but it was cold and foamy, and he smiled and smacked his lips at his first sip. I stored my confusing thoughts about the lobby guy in the back of my brain and asked, "Were the three of you on the *Iwo Jima* together, or did you meet at the reunion?"

17

Steve answered my question, "The reunion. We were all on the *Iwo*, but at different times and never met. The Navy doesn't usually hold reunions in non-sailor towns, but this time they were honoring a veteran. When I heard they'd made an exception, I made sure to attend. We sat at the same table for dinner both nights and struck up a friendship when we figured out that we all lived in Hunter. Carlee and I haven't lived there long, so it was nice to meet a few neighbors and fellow sailors. Gus and Phyllis, who have cruised about everywhere, call themselves cruisomaniacs and told us about this repositioning cruise to Portugal. Carlee and I decided to make it a foursome, and now that you have made it a sixsome, it's even better. I thought the cruise would be sold out, but we were able to book rooms, even obtain a room with a balcony. How about you, Griff, did you get a balcony?"

Griff shrugged his shoulders. "I don't know if we did or not. I didn't ask, and they didn't tell." He squeezed my shoulder and chuckled at his little Navy joke.

I ignored Griff's attempted humor saying, "I'm glad to know our destination. Griff forgot to ask and thought it might be Paris or Barcelona. I was hoping Paris, so I could practice my French, but it doesn't matter because I've never traveled much, and I'm happy to go anywhere to get away from this year's cold and snow. We've never cruised before, and we will have to learn the ropes. Should we have requested a balcony?"

"They cost a little more than a cabin without a balcony, but yes, definitely you should request an upgrade and with any luck the cruise line will upgrade you for free, although you might have to pay extra," Gus warned.

I heard the words *cost a little more* and *pay extra* and figured my chickens were cooked, we would definitely be in steerage. When I told Griff the cost of the first-class flight, it had almost done him in, but I fibbed and told him only the cost for one of us, not two. What he didn't know, well, he didn't have to know.

Gus continued, "No matter, you'll appreciate having a balcony to sit in the sun and watch the world go by." He continued in a half-whisper, "And another little benefit: you've heard of *sex on the beach*? That's a neon-colored vodka drink, but you'll never have anything sexier than *sea sex on the balcony*. And when the ocean spray hits your naked bodies, good, erotic balcony sex compares to nothing else. Phyllis loves it." Gus laughed out loud and chuckled, "Don't you, Phyllis?"

I glanced in the direction he had spoken and saw a substantial woman with a large goblet of something blue with a paper umbrella and a slice of pineapple protruding from its lip, ambling up to the table. She greeted us with a huge smile, "Griff! Hi, I'm surprised to see you. I thought you didn't like cruises." She looked at me and nodded, "You must be Griff's BFF? I'm Phyllis Gustafson, Gus' wife." A silver charm bracelet dangled from her wrist, as she reached out her puffy hand sliding her fingers across my palm.

"What's a BFF?" I asked, never having heard the term.

"Text talk, like the kids do, Best Friend Forever," Phyllis answered without missing a beat. "I'm happy to meet you. Griff is a charmer, but you probably made him that way."

"What's that blue drink, Phyllis, blueberry Kool-Aid?" Griff asked.

"No, it's called a blue Hawaiian, and it's yummy," Phyllis laughed. "It's an entire day's FDA fruit supply in one glass, made with coconut and pineapple and loaded with nutrients, and it prevents almost everything that could affect us senior citizens. You know how we seniors have to watch what we eat." She paused adding with a laugh, "And the rum and curacao give it a big kick in the patootie. You should try it, Audrey."

I liked Phyllis immediately. She had an amicable way about her that perked me up and gave me hope our trip might be okay after all. Her laughter echoed throughout the room, causing people to turn and smile, even though they had no idea why she was laughing. She weighed less than Gus, but even so, she soaked up a vast amount of chair space. At around five-foot-seven, she carried the weight of a person four inches taller, but it didn't seem to bother her. She was confident and optimistic. And funny. Dressed in a red and yellow flowered muumuu, leather strappy sandals, and carrying a huge clear plastic handbag on her shoulder, she had mastered the tourist look. She finished off the devil-may-care style by gathering her silvery blonde, curly hair into an uncooperative ponytail with large curly bangs spilling over her eyebrows. Her blue-framed half-glasses that sat on the end of her nose had been smudged by the wayward pineapple slice.

"Audrey changed my mind, and we decided to chance it. She can be an extremely convincing woman," Griff told Phyllis.

I didn't quite recall the conversation the same way he did because I had been a footnote in his decision. Of course, I wouldn't have argued because this year's winter in Hunter had been especially brutal, snowing forty-seven days in a row. Most days I was trapped in the house as driving had become difficult, some days even impossible. It took an act of God to get the county to plow our road, and I sensed despondency digging in on those days when I couldn't drive the twenty miles to the store or library or even collect the mail at the end of our driveway. It was so cold even my pedometer froze, and I fell far beneath my 10,000-step goal. This pushed my loneliness into depression, and although I looked for ways out of it, the isolation on most days hovered throughout my heart and soul.

I was nursing a glass of white wine when I glimpsed the white-haired gentleman enter the bar and seat himself near the server's station. The server handed him something in a stemmed glass, maybe a martini, as he continued to look my way. Our eyes locked for a full minute, until I forced them to look elsewhere. I idly wondered if he would be on the cruise to Lisbon. Not that it mattered. I did not look his way again until a waiter set a second glass of Chardonnay in front of me, saying, "With compliments of the gentleman at the end of the bar." My eyes skimmed the bar from end to end, but I didn't see him. *What was his name? Logan something? Hill? No, Hall, Logan Hall.* Just then, I saw him peek out from behind the wait station area. He raised his glass as if toasting me and winked. My breasts tightened, and I stopped breathing for a moment, hoping Griff didn't notice.

But Griff did notice. He saw everything. He saw Logan's wink and tightened his arm around me, drawing me closer, as if claiming me, like a prize. I looked up at Griff and shifted my eyes to view Logan, wondering. Wondering about everything but saying nothing.

# CHAPTER 8
## *Audrey*

It was March, and the Idaho weather had exhausted my positive outlook of winter, but in Fort Lauderdale the sun shined, and warm gusts of ocean wind ricocheted from building to building. I had worn slacks and a sweater for the early morning flight, but Fort Lauderdale was a warm seventy-five, nearly fifty degrees warmer than it had been in Idaho, and I was glad to have changed into cooler clothing to board the ship. Griff likewise donned tan shorts and a green and white polo shirt with his black socks and stained tennis shoes.

We had retreated from the group the night before and made our way back to our tiny room. "This balcony is small, but it might work for Gus' suggestion of *sex on the balcony*. What do you think?" Griff suggested.

"I don't think so. Gus was talking about sea sex, spelled s-e-a, which might be okay on the ship, we can talk about it later, but here, on this balcony with people in tall buildings looking down, it would be s-e-e sex for everyone in these buildings to see. It's not going to happen." I cringed at the thought.

Griff shrugged and replied, "I still think it's a good idea, don't get all huffy."

I went inside and grimaced as I stared at our colorless legs, "If I had known we were cruising, I would have visited the tanning salon. Our pasty white limbs need color, so hopefully we will get some sun on the trip. Wouldn't you like to buy a pair of sandals before we head out? And maybe a couple new pairs of shorts?" I asked Griff. "Your feet might get hot in those tennis shoes, and since they trekked through the barn and manure all winter, they kinda stink."

He looked down at them and sniffed, "They stink? I didn't notice. I've never bought a pair of sandals in my life, but now that I think about it, maybe a sandal would fit over my bunion better. How's that for being spontaneous? I should have seen a foot doctor before this trip. Let's go have breakfast, and then we'll follow it up with a little shopping trip."

Griff and I rode the elevator to the first floor where the Crystal Café was located. Phyllis and Gus saw us enter and waved us over. We ordered coffee and orange juice from the server and stood in line for the Kit and Caboodle Buffet, whatever that meant.

I chose cottage cheese and one slice of bacon, and Griff selected sausage, eggs, hash browns, orange slices, and toast. He leaned over whispering, "The hotel included breakfast in the price, so we should load up. You should grab more food because God knows what they'll feed us on the ship. Gus told me the food was good but what if it antagonizes my gout?"

"You have gout? You never told me that," I responded.

Griff shook his head, "I don't yet, but I might if I eat rich food. Do you remember my friend Sam? He has gout and can't ski anymore. And I don't want to mess things up and have to swallow more damn pills."

"You haven't skied since you retired, and you already take a bunch of pills, so what difference would one more make?" I reasoned.

By the time we returned to the table, the bussers had removed Gus and Phyllis' dishes, but Gus had made a return trip to the serving bar for another cinnamon roll and banana. Phyllis reprimanded him with her eyes but pinched off a large piece of the cinnamon roll for herself. "Dang, these rolls taste good," Gus salivated. "Amazing. They have a hint of orange in them. Vitamin C. I read that OJ has oodles of calories, in fact, this sweet roll might have fewer calories than a glass of OJ."

Phyllis laughed at Gus' comments, "No, a cinnamon roll has more calories than OJ, but we can look it up in the diet book the doc gave me. I brought it along, and we can check after we board the ship and unpack."

Gus exclaimed, "Diet book? You brought a diet book with you? You must be kidding. Does that mean you're planning to lecture me on every goddam thing I put in my mouth this whole goddam trip?"

"No, Gus, I won't be lecturing you. Your doc handed me this book to review. You can put whatever you want in your goddam mouth, do what you want, but you know what the docs have been telling you: Get rid of the gut," Phyllis answered.

"I hate dieting," Gus told me, shaking his head. "Hey, Steve, Carlee, come and join us."

"Good morning, all," Steve greeted. "The breakfast bar looks amazing. Audrey, I want you to meet my wife, Carlee."

Carlee, a tall, shapely woman, held a goblet of OJ in her hand. Her jet-black hair was chopped into a shag, protruding out in several directions and held in place with a black rhinestone headband. Dressed in black shorts, t-shirt, and high-heeled wedged sandals, she contrasted her fashion with a paisley, magenta silk scarf looping her neck and silver hoops dangling from her ears. She lined her dusty rose lipstick with black and shaded her eyes with black and purple mascara and liner. I thought she had probably been attractive as a young woman, but now was plagued with dry skin that made deep wrinkles in her face, neck, and hands. The wrinkles could have been caused by excess sun, but I had observed the dry skin of alcoholics in my work at the treatment center and wondered if too much of the bottle had been a contributing factor for her, too.

She stretched across Griff's chest where she rested her palm and wagged her fingers toward me cooing, "So pleased to meet you, Audrey, you have a fascinating husband, and we are delighted the two of you could join us."

"Yes, I'm pleased to meet you, too. We missed you last night, I hope you feel better," I said, eyeing the goblet, wondering if it contained just OJ or had she also added a splash or two of vodka?

Griff announced, "I'm going to stretch my legs and find a shoe store. Audrey said she'd rather stay behind to pack up our clothes. Does anybody else need shoes?"

Carlee answered quickly, "Shoe store? Sure, I'll go. The strip mall located about a block from here has a good shoe store, so how about I take you there while Steve repacks our suitcases? I want to check out the shoes, too. A new pair of sandals for the cruise can't hurt, right? Steve, could you also check with the front desk to confirm van space for the six of us at eleven o'clock? That will allow us to be at the pier by noon. The ship allows us to carry one bottle of wine for each person, so I'll buy two for us. Anybody else want wine?" Carlee linked her arm through Griff's and breathed, "Do you mind? Wedges can be wobbly, and I want to steady myself."

Steve answered, "What about breakfast? Aren't you going to have a bite to eat?"

Carlee smiled widely, "No, I'll go with Griff. I can easily grab something to eat at the bakery. Give me a sec while I pour my OJ into a paper cup."

I agreed, "Yes, that would be nice. Griff, would you buy us a couple bottles of wine, too. I prefer white, but anything works."

Griff uncharacteristically gave me a high five, "Okay, Hon, it's all set. Shoes and wine followed by the adventure of a lifetime."

# CHAPTER 9
## *Audrey*

Phyllis spied a wheelchair as we exited the hotel's van and announced, "Gus, I requested a wheelchair for me for embarkation. You know those ramps can be tricky for me. We're all together, meaning they'll let us board as one unit, and if I'm in a wheelchair, we will move more quickly if we pass through the *handicapped only* gate." She plunked herself down in the nearest wheelchair and hefted their two carry-on bags and her huge handbag onto her lap. She balanced his cane on top of the pile and breathed out, "Okay, Gus, wheel!"

With Gus pushing Phyllis and their bags, we slowly zigzagged through and around and under the directional tape to the *handicapped only* gate where a shorter line formed, but still had a dozen small groups in various stages of disability, including canes, walkers, wheelchairs, and electric scooters. Carry-on bags and a few extra assistive devices accompanied the queue as they inched toward the cruise staff and ship security.

Griff carried our two bottles of wine while I secured our documents in the purse I had slung across my chest. I had checked in everything else and had no other luggage to carry on. Griff leaned over and whispered, "I've heard cruises are called wrinkle and crinkle trips, and now I know why. Everybody except us is wrinkly and crinkly, well, I know that I'm not any way, but I'm not sure about you," he teased. "Just kidding, Aud, you look fantastic, and I'm looking forward to tonight. I keep remembering what Gus mentioned about sea-sex, and I can't wait to try it."

My mind flashed to the gentleman in the lobby, and I turned my head to see if he was in line, relieved he was not. *Get him out of your mind*, I demanded of myself. *What's wrong with me? Griff loves me, and I... well, I won't throw out all these years of marriage.* I took a deep breath and responded to Griff, "We don't even know if we have a balcony or not."

Carlee and Steve settled in as the caboose of the group, wrestling their carry-on luggage, one small suitcase, one backpack, and two small duffels. Without warning, Steve set the suitcase and duffels on the floor, attached the backpack to his back, touched his ears a few times, and began rifling through his pockets. He opened the suitcase, followed by the duffel bags and backpack and pulled everything out, then dumped it back into the containers. Carlee cradled a duffle containing the two bottles of wine in her arms as if she feared they would break, "What are you doing, Steve? Did you lose something?"

He touched his ears as he kicked their bags forward. As the line inched ahead, he whispered, "I can't find my damn hearing aids. I had them this morning, but I must have left them in the room. Dammit, I can't hear anything without them. Look in your purse."

Carlee quickly answered, "Why are you just noticing this now? You've been with the group for hours and only now you realize you can't hear?"

Steve, not appreciating the reprimand, started to look inside Carlee's purse.

"Steve, what are doing? I'm sure they are not in my purse because I took it with me to buy our wine. We can check our carry-ons again, but maybe you packed them in the big suitcase. I'll call the hotel to ask whether you left them in the room and request that they bring them to us before the ship leaves in two hours. Plenty of time," she remarked, digging through her purse for her phone. She found the number online, dialed it, and told the desk clerk about their problem. "What do you mean you don't have us registered? Your van brought us to the pier before noon. We stayed in room 672."

"No, ma'am, we don't have you registered in room 672. You must have been at a different hotel," the agent answered curtly.

"I have the receipt in my hand, Ritzy-Que Hotel, Room 672. Steven Sanderson. $218.00."

"You have called the Ritzy-Que, but I'm sorry, Ma'am. We registered no one named Steve Sanderson last night."

Carlee clicked off and related the story to Steve and the rest of us. "Unbelievable," Steve commented. "What do we do?"

"I'll try again in a few minutes. Maybe she was new," Carlee replied. "We have to find them."

Twenty minutes later, we arrived at the cruise agent's desk with Phyllis and Gus leading, followed by Griff and me. Steve continued to comb through the pockets of his shorts for his hearing aids but found nothing but lint and a leftover breath mint.

The cruise agent requested our tickets, passports, IDs, and a credit card, which Griff begrudgingly pulled from his wallet saying, "I already paid for the cruise. What do you need this for?"

The agent smiled and answered, "Incidentals, Honey, in case you forgot something, such as toothpaste, or if you want to order a glass of wine or a margarita."

"I'm sure Audrey packed toothpaste, but okay because she'll undoubtedly want a margarita, or one of those blue Hawaii things. By the way, do we have a balcony? My friends suggested we request a balcony. Where is our room?" Griff asked.

"You're in room 3-013 on the third deck, no balcony, but it has a window. As far as I know, we are completely booked but you can request a room change at the front desk and maybe someone will want to switch rooms. Okay, I have checked you in," she handed Griff his credit card and the ship ID cards.

"Does the window open?" Griff asked. "I want windows that open if we can't get a balcony."

"No, your window won't open because you would probably get wet and the ocean can be chilly," the agent answered. "And you never know about those flying fish."

I asked, "What about our passports? We need our passports, don't we?"

"Is this your first cruise, Honey? Don't worry, we'll take good care of them and return them when you disembark. We'll take them to the ports of entry and have them stamped with the various countries we visit, too. Have a great cruise."

The long, winding ramp to the ship sloped gently, and we all trudged across the dock toward its entry. Gus continued to push the wheelchair but had slowed down and began to pant. Phyllis asked, "Are you okay, Gus? Do we need to swap places for the rest of the way? I can make it from here. You are sweating, and I don't want you to have a heart attack. Using a wheelchair definitely makes embarkation quicker, but I can walk."

Gus wiped a few beads of perspiration off his brow and shook his head. "No, I'm fine. I'm sure we're about there. I think it's your charm bracelet weighing me down, but I can do it."

Behind me, I heard Carlee assuring Steve, "We will call the hotel again the minute we get on the ship, if we have cell service, that is. Maybe we can talk to a different desk clerk who could better help us. We still have a while until we set sail."

Griff stared at the windows in the massive ship and counted three floors up from the water line. In his scrutinizing eyes, the round windows measured about twelve inches in diameter. He frowned at me as he noticed, "Those windows are smaller than a good cow pie. This cruise will last two weeks, so we're gonna need to change rooms."

We boarded the ship leaving the wheelchair behind and accepted a glass of complimentary *Welcome Aboard!* champagne. Gus and Phyllis located a cart for their luggage, and Carlee and Steve beelined it to their room to phone the hotel, hoping to locate Steve's hearing aids.

Griff and I climbed a flight of stairs to the front desk only to encounter another line. Griff's impatience had escalated to *Let's go back to Hunter,* so I volunteered to hold our place in line and suggested he find a beer. He said, "I'll be back in a few minutes. Get us a new room, no matter what." He handed me the paper bag containing two bottles of wine and headed out. We hadn't moved in several minutes, but as soon as the front desk added two clerks, the lines began to move quickly, and I suddenly found myself next in line. Where was Griff?

## CHAPTER 10
### *Steve*

Steve and Carlee carried their bags to the assigned cabin and dumped everything onto the bed. Steve re-searched everything while Carlee phoned the Ritzy-Que. A different hotel clerk answered the phone, and Carlee repeated her story.

"No, Ma'am, we didn't find any hearing aids. In fact, room 672 was vacant last night. Do you have the right hotel?" the clerk asked politely.

Carlee spat out, "Yes, dammit. We stayed at the Ritzy-Que last night. Why can't you find our reservation? Could you look again? Steven Sanderson. $218."

The clerk listened to Carlee and responded, "Uh, hold on for a second, I want to check something."

The clerk came back on the phone in less than a minute, "Okay, Ma'am, I can tell you what happened. The Ritz Z Inn Corporation built two Ritzy-Ques only one block apart on the same street, 1452 N. James and 1462 N. James, so you can see the confusion. I checked the other Ritzy-Que and indeed you were their guest last night. You can call them to ask about your misplaced hearing aids." She recited the phone number to Carlee.

Steve heard what the clerk told Carlee and growled, "I'm going to the bar while you sort this out. Tell them to bring my hearing aids here because we will be leaving shortly, and I can't leave the ship."

"Bring me a drink, wine or vodka tonic," Carlee requested, dialing the number of the other hotel. They placed her on hold, caller number

29

six. She waited and listened to elevator music as the minutes dragged by. It was a long wait to be connected, yet the same minutes raced by until their departure for Portugal. Finally, an apparently harried clerk named Lila answered, and Carlee retold her story for the third time.

Lila said, "Yes, Ma'am, we registered you and your husband last night, but we haven't cleaned room 672 yet, so I don't know if you left your lost articles in the room. I can call you back if we locate the hearing aids, and you can come and reclaim them at your leisure."

"Our leisure? What the hell are you talking about? Listen, Lila, we need them now because we will leave on a two-week cruise in less than an hour. I'll remain on the phone while you send somebody to the room to look for the hearing aids. If they are in the room, and I believe they are, you can Uber them to the ship and bring them to us. You can charge the Uber ride to our credit card, no problem. You have about forty-three minutes to get them here. We'll wait by the gate and grab them when you arrive. Now go, I'm staying on the phone."

Lila held the phone in her hand, noticed the growing line of check-ins and check-outs in front of her and caught the eye of her supervisor. "You aren't going to believe what they want us to do," Lila told him, repeating Carlee's instructions.

"I'll go upstairs and check," the supervisor offered. "What room?"

"762," Lila told him, without verifying the room number on her computer screen. "762."

The supervisor, Henry, headed toward the elevator, dodging guests and luggage in the lobby. He rode the elevator to the seventh floor and tapped on room 762's door, simultaneously using his key card to access the room. A loud "whaddyawant" reverberated through the door, and Henry stopped his entrance and checked the room number. 762. He used his radio to call Lila at the front desk.

"You said room 762, right?" Henry asked.

"No, 672, sixth floor, not seventh," Lila responded flatly after looking at the computer screen again.

"Okay, I thought you said 762, but it still has guests in the room."

Henry descended by stairs to the sixth floor and rapped loudly on the door, at the same time pressing his master key against the access pad. *Right room, thank God,* he thought. On the bedside table, amid two used tissues and wadded up piece of paper, lay the two hearing aids. Not wanting to touch them, he grabbed a tissue from the bathroom to wrap and deposit them in his shirt pocket. He verified the time. Twenty-seven minutes until the ship leaves, and the pier lies only twelve minutes away. Fifteen minutes, plenty of time.

He dashed out of the building punching numbers on his phone. "The pier," he snapped at the Uber driver.

The Uber driver didn't move, but asked, "Which pier? What boat? Currently eight ships are in the harbor. Which one?"

Henry didn't know and dialed Lila's cell number. "I found that guy's ear gizmos, but where am I taking them? I'm in an Uber on my way to the pier."

"Hold on, she's still on the phone, I'll ask her," Lila barked. "Ma'am, which ship are you on? We have the hearing aids, and my supervisor found an Uber to go to the pier, but we don't know which pier, or which ship."

Carlee was sipping her vodka tonic, not tuning in to Lila's question, but thanked her profusely, "We appreciate your doing this, and you've been so helpful and kind, thank you."

Lila, clearly irritated, spat out, "Don't hang up, Ma'am. Which pier and which ship? Ma'am?"

"Oh, I'm not sure. The ship is *The Broadwater,* but I don't know which pier. I didn't pay attention when we boarded. It might have been four or maybe seven. No, it must have been three. The terminal was an enormous gray building with lots of people outside, guests and crew, but I'm unsure of the number," Carlee returned. Just then, she heard a ship's whistle blow. "Tell him to hurry."

Lila relayed the information to Henry, and the Uber driver began weaving his way through the traffic toward the dozen piers providing guest services to enter and exit port. Taxis and Ubers and vans and busses jammed the streets, and the traffic crept toward the port entry.

The Uber driver commented, "I've seen *The Broadwater*. It's a silver ship with a blue waterfall painted on its bow, if I recall correctly."

"It's back there," Henry declared, pointing the opposite direction. "Three piers down." The driver flipped a U-turn, causing several middle fingers to extend toward the Uber, and Henry checked his watch again: four minutes to go but traffic had stopped.

The ship's crew began to hoist the entry steps and remove the ropes tethering it to the pier. Henry could see hundreds of cruising guests celebrating their *bon voyage* party, waving and shouting from the main deck and sky deck, most with drinks in their hands. He jumped out of the Uber, shouting, "Wait for me, I'll be right back," and ran the fifty yards toward the untethered ship that slowly drifted toward the open sea, yet had only moved inches from the pier.

Steve stood on the main deck and noticed the young man in the brown and gold Ritzy Que uniform racing toward the ship and shouted, "Here! Here! Do you have my hearing aids? Throw them to me, and I'll catch them."

Henry stared at Steve standing at the ship's rail, waving his arms and shouting as he watched the ship gliding away from the pier. It was now about a foot away and both thought it would be an easy toss.

Henry yanked the devices from his shirt pocket, and they spilled from the tissue to the dock. He scooped them up in his hand and posed to toss them when he realized the ship had floated six additional feet. "Damn," Steve and Henry shouted simultaneously, their unheard words wafting into the ocean air.

# CHAPTER 11
## *Audrey*

I was aware that a balcony room would be more expensive, and with Griff's continued focus on our financial situation, I would have preferred Griff to accompany me to choose our new room, should one be available, but now he was nowhere in sight. I shifted the wine from one arm to the other before moving toward the smiling agent.

I sighed, "As first-time cruisers, we mistakenly purchased a cabin without a balcony, but we would prefer having fresh air. Do you have any balcony cabins available? My husband has health issues and will be claustrophobic in our assigned room, Room 3-013," I fibbed. He wasn't claustrophobic, but I knew he would be unhappy in the smaller room. "And 3-013 is an evil number. We can't stay in there because in my church three means death and thirteen is unlucky." Would God strike me dead for that lie?

The agent listened carefully, pretending to understand, "We understand, and you're in luck because a guest canceled a few minutes ago. We can place you in a two-room suite. It's our last available accommodation, but it costs more, in fact double the cost of Cabin 3-013. Do you still want it?"

I glanced toward the entrance, searching for Griff, *no matter what* echoing in my brain, "That would be wonderful, we'll take it," I agreed. "I don't want to know the price, please charge it to our credit card." *No matter what.* If I heard the price, I would change my mind.

"Fine," the young agent answered. "You'll have to sign a new contract to change the rooms, but your luggage will be automatically transferred.

Your new room, number 10-021, comes with an oversized balcony and a lovely sitting area for you and your husband. In addition, you will have access to the Platinum Lounge where you can have private meals and complimentary nosh and drinks. The lounge lies three or four doors down from your room and is available now. Believe me, you're gonna be a happy woman."

"Nosh and drinks, yes, it sounds lovely. We'll take it," I agreed. I had no idea what nosh was, but it sounded good and was complimentary. Griff would approve of anything complimentary. Still, I scanned the crowd, hoping to locate him and suggest we view the cabin together. Knowing Griff's current obsession with sex, he would probably lobby to go belly to belly right now, but I'd risk it. Maybe I could divert him with whatever nosh was.

I heard a voice behind me, but next to my ear, "Well, hello again. Audrey, right? Did you manage to find a husband?"

It was Logan, standing in the adjacent line, waiting to speak with a desk clerk. I turned toward him, and his friendly brown eyes and mysterious smile caught me by surprise. I sucked in a deep breath, almost a gasp, and my lower deck turned flipflops again. My college friends had talked about men with *bedroom eyes,* but I had no idea what they meant until now, half a century later. As his eyes charmed me, my breasts tightened and popped up front and center, Barbie doll style. I had a flashing, scary thought that my size 36B bra had burst its seams trying to contain my newly enlarged breasts, which I think had expanded to a size 40D. My eyes wanted to take a peek toward his crotch, but I willed myself to blink and moved my gaze to his left ear, but believe me, it wasn't that easy.

Logan Hall indeed experienced the same sensations. He raised and lowered his weight to his toes, trying to keep from having his own physical reaction. He forced himself to calm down and asked, "May I buy you a glass of wine? I'll be finished here in two seconds; I'm getting my key card punched because I don't want to lose it. I recommend you get punched, too, and use a lanyard to keep your card safe."

34

My body was an out-of-control fire and words fell out of my mouth faster than a springtime mountain stream, but I managed to say, "Punched? No, thank you, I don't want to be punched."

Logan started to respond, but I interrupted him, "Oh, you mean get my room card punched. Okay, I'll get punched. I mean, I don't mean I'll get punched; I mean I'll get my key card punched. I must be babbling again. No, thank you, you already bought me a glass at the hotel. I mean a glass of wine. I need to go, I'm late to see my husband in the barn."

"No problem," he laughed, "we can do it another time, and I'll be happy to foot the bill for drinks for both you and your husband. Get it? Foot the bill, I'm a podiatrist."

I giggled at his joke, "Really, a podiatrist? Boarding the ship and standing in line to get a larger room has taken its toll on me. My husband went someplace, and he needs a bunion for his foot, but I'm not sure where he went, probably at a barn, uh, I mean probably at a bar. He has new sandals."

"That's nice," Logan said amused. I am not sure how I was keeping him so entertained.

Now, not only was my lower forty on fire, but my emotions had been either thrown in a pool of water or tumbled into an abyss, I wasn't sure which, but my brain told me I needed to slow down. "I, that is Griff and I, can access the Platinum Lounge, and meet there for a drink later, if you'd like. The drinks are free, and I'm sure Griff would enjoy sharing his bunions with you, especially since you know about bunions."

"Thank you, but I don't think they will let me into the Platinum," Logan said frowning.

"Why? Because you're black? That's against the law," I said, emphatically.

"I am? I hadn't noticed," he teased, his eyes twinkling. "No, they won't let me in because they'll only allow you to enter the private lounges if you stay in a suite, but I'm in third class, sixth floor."

"Why don't we see for ourselves? We could test it out before Griff joins us. I'll tell them you're my husband, and they won't know the difference," I blurted out before I thought. I didn't know if I was thinking quickly or my brain had shut down. So much for slowing down.

*Why did I say that? What would Griff say?*

## CHAPTER 12
### *Griff*

The Rising Tide Lounge, decorated with brass rails, bamboo tables, and flowered chairs and couches hinted at the Caribbean. The costumed wait staff encouraged tropical drinks and hors d'oeuvres. Griff, Gus, and Phyllis had settled into the lounge to wait for the others and had been waiting for an hour or more without seeing anyone except the bartender, a few bar drifters, and a blue bird sitting on the floor. A tall, dark-haired man, apparently blind, sat at the bar nursing a Bloody Mary. His vested and harnessed service dog sat beside him.

Griff, a true dog lover, rose to speak with the man and the dog and came back to report the service dog was a black Lab/pointer mix. The dog had a graying snout, and gray front paws, and drank water from a small dish.

Gus asked, "What's the guy's story? Is he blind?"

"Apparently. I didn't ask him, but his name is Mel Black, and his dog is Jack. He said he's from Great Falls, Montana. He might be former military because of the short hair, but he didn't say as much. I was surprised they let dogs on cruise ships," Griff said.

Gus explained, "They allow service dogs, especially if the passenger is blind, but probably not any other dogs. Our sea time for this cruise to Lisbon is about five days, plus another five in various ports, a long time for a dog to be on the water."

Griff and Gus had each consumed two beers, and Phyllis drank two tall glasses of water before she changed the subject, "Our doctor suggested that Gus and I pay more attention to our diet, not go on a diet, rather a lifestyle change," Phyllis told the others. "His recommendation is called YBFAT Lifestyle, an acronym for Young, Bright, Fit, and Thin, and it focuses on vegetables and protein, similar to the Keto stuff, only better. It helps with weight, fitness, and brain power through adjusting eating and living habits. You drink a gallon of water, read or do puzzles twenty minutes a day, walk twenty minutes, and sleep at least eight hours a night. Oh, and not more than one alcoholic drink. But I'm on a vacation, I mean, I'm going to try, but it seems impossible to make a lifestyle change while on vacation."

Gus rolled his eyes, "I'm not drinking a gallon of water every day. No way and anyway, I'm also on vacation. Diets are for the birds. So many promises, but no results. We don't yo-yo diet, we bungee diet. Moderation, that's the best way. Besides, Phyl, I love you the way you are."

"Your doctor recommended it, and you need to listen to him. You used to be slim and trim and built for speed, but no longer. Your tummy bounces when you walk, and you're out of breath at the least exertion, like today, when you wheeled me up the ramp. The fitter Gus of yesteryear would not be sucking wind like Secretariat," Phyllis reached over and gave him a Pillsbury Doughboy punch in his ample breadbasket and flirted, "I want you around until we're both decrepit. So, what do you say? Okie, dokey, my cute hokey pokey? Let's change our lifestyle together, cut the beer and wine, drink more water, and start sleeping and reading more. How about you, Griff, you're our age and don't have a growing gut. How do you do it?"

Griff grinned as he looked from Gus to Phyllis and rolled out an easy answer, "Launching the meat missile, three times a day, morning, noon, and night. That'll do it."

Gus asked hesitantly, "Launching the meat missile? Which means...?"

"Doing the dirty...dipping the wick...wonking the willy...in plain words, sex, three times a day."

"Oh, my," Phyllis giggled as she flicked her charm bracelet to make it tinkle. "Three times a day? You're gonna make me blush, Griff."

Gus laughed, "It sounds unusual, but, hey, if it works for you, maybe we should try it, Phyl, making us both fit instead of fat." He cracked a wide smile, fisted his hands, and pumped them back and forth while repeating, "Chugga, chugga, chugga, chugga."

Steve and Carlee entered the bar, and Gus waved them over. They sat down on the extended couch between Gus and Griff, who increased his voice volume to ask, "How's the hunt for the hearing aids going? Did you hear anything yet?"

"Very funny, Griff. You won't believe this, but it's classic. The hotel found them, and the hotel dope had them in his hand but dropped them, and the ship floated out of reach while he bent down to pick them up, so, no, I didn't get them, and now I'll be saying *what* or *huh* the whole damn cruise," Steve replied. "I missed getting them by two or three feet."

Phyllis asked, "Two or three feet? Couldn't you reach that far?"

Steve looked puzzled, "Reach the bar? We weren't in the bar; we were on the deck, trying to stretch to the pier. Maybe he was afraid he would fall into the bay. It's a bummer, a real bummer for me, and I don't know if I'll get them back or if he'll trash them."

"It's hard. Not being able to hear will make both of us go bonkers," Carlee commented, looked at Griff and asked, "Where's Audrey? Did you get your third-floor cabin swapped for one with a balcony?"

"I haven't seen her yet. I left her at the front desk to deal with it, but maybe she's lost or still trying to figure it out; she had at least a dozen people ahead of her. I told her to do whatever it takes, and she might have needed to negotiate, have them move other people, or pay a little more. She'll find us when she gets done," Griff answered, nodding.

"I heard the ship was filled, no extra available cabins," Carlee reported, placing her hand on Griff's arm.

"She's smart and will figure it out," Griff replied, patting Carlee's hand. "She's as reliable as Coors buying my hops crop. She'll make it happen."

## CHAPTER 13
### *Audrey*

The Platinum Lounge was private and chic. I dug out my cruise card and located our names on the guest list and initialed both my name and Griff's. A female attendant named Katrin greeted us and invited us to sit wherever we wanted. She offered to bring us drinks, complimentary, of course. Rattled at being with a person other than Griff, I intended to order a glass of Merlot, but the word *martini* exited my mouth instead. Logan asked for a glass of wine, anything he said. I had never had a martini before.

The Platinum was a small, cozy room walled with books, paintings, and an array of food and drinks. Another area included a settee and a couple of small tables. A few small statues and lamps sat on the tables, and the settee held bright colored pillows and throws.

We were the only guests in the lounge. I began fidgeting, and my wit remained witless. "I shouldn't be here; I should find Griff. I don't even know you," I mentioned to Logan. More senseless words flew out of my mouth, "I'm married, and my friends and my husband are waiting for me to tell him about our new suite. I shouldn't be there, I mean here." The attendant brought cheese, crackers, and nuts, which we both ignored.

"Why not? You are your own person, who happens to be unbelievably appealing, and he probably won't mind your having a drink or two before we join him," Logan commented, flashing a smile.

"Two? No, I shouldn't even have one," I pleaded, "I'm a little uneasy. I told hostess Katrin you are my husband, which you're not, and now you seem to be hitting on me. What would my kids say? Or my husband for that matter?"

Logan tilted his head a bit and broadened his smile, "I know we just met, and I must seem forward to you, but frankly, I don't care. I can't recall ever having been attracted to any woman as strongly as I am drawn to you, not even my wife."

*This could lead to a disaster.* "You're married?" I almost shouted, looking over at Katrin, who had an amused look on her face, so I toned my voice down, "That's even worse."

My eyes must have popped out of my head because he said, "No, relax, Audrey, not anymore. Joan died four years ago after a long bout with diabetes. We were married for thirty-eight years. We can relax for a few minutes, can't we?" Logan reached for my hand, cradling it in his. "You have lovely hands, but the first things I noticed about you were your exquisite, even sexy feet. Perfect toes, perfect ankles. Sexy."

I yanked my hand away, feeling awkward and cautious. I hadn't been attracted to a man other than Griff in decades and certainly hadn't gained the attention of anyone besides Griff in at least that long. I needed to leave, but didn't want to be rude, so I changed the subject, "You're a podiatrist? That's an odd specialty. Why did you choose feet?" I asked, gulping down the last of my martini.

Logan chuckled, "I like feet. I like how they look, what they do, how they move, and even how they smell."

The martini had worked fast, and I asked, "So, you are saying you like felly smeet?" as Katrin handed me another martini, this time in a larger glass. I giggled as I corrected myself, "smelly feet." I took another drink.

Logan nodded at Katrin and said, "Thank you." He laughed aloud, "Actually, no. I don't care much for smelly feet, but I do get a kick out of the foot issues with funny names: Grandpa's toes, hammer toe, bunions, heel spurs, warts, corns, athlete's foot, and claw toes, to name a few. After all these years of dealing with feet, the names still make me laugh, although the health issues surrounding them can be difficult, even life-changing, they do have comical names. Shortly after Joan and I married, her doctor diagnosed diabetes, and through the years she had multiple foot issues, leading to amputation of three toes shortly before she retired, and I had a nephew born with a club foot. Feet have been part of my life, in multiple ways, forever. You see, I even have two of them," he lifted his feet in the air and shook them.

"Griff is a bunion," I interjected, the martini continuing to mess with my brain. "And he says he's getting worse, so maybe he should see a podiatrist to get it minimized or removed. And he's worried about gout. Is gout related to feet?"

"Are you asking me for free medical advice? I don't work for free, but I might barter. Do you have something to trade?" Logan answered picking up my hand again. "Lady Luck smiled at me when I decided to go on this cruise and now, here you are," he said continuing to caress each finger in turn. "I hadn't planned this trip, but a flier came in the mail, and I didn't have anything better to do so I signed on the dotted line. I have two daughters who live on the east coast, Jan and Laura Lee, and they constantly advise me I am crumbly and falling apart at my advanced age, but I reminded them I don't have one *foot* in the grave and have itchy *feet*, so I put my *foot* down. My daughters groan at my foot jokes, but they know they'll inherit my money when I'm six *feet* under."

I emitted a hiccup and began to giggle at his foot jokes. By now, I was giggling at almost anything, and said, "You must have a *footlocker* full of foot jokes. I can't go *toe to toe* with you, but I'll put my best *foot* forward." Sometime during our banter, my hand made its way into his again, but I plucked it away and looked at my watch. By the time I finished my second martini, we had been in the Platinum for nearly an hour. The time had zoomed by, but I knew Griff would be wondering where I was. My head was swimming with disconnected and smutty thoughts, but I was not completely out of it. I knew if I stayed any longer, I would be tempted to have a third, and my martinis might become martoonis, and who knew what would happen. I was a married woman, and Logan was clearly interested in me. I needed to pull myself together. "This has been fun, Logan, but I'm not footloose and fancy free, and I need to make tracks to find my husband and give him the key to our room. Would you join me? I'd like you to meet Griff and our friends."

As we left the Platinum Lounge, he surprised me, cradling my face in two hands and kissing my cheek whispering, "I know I've come on fast, but I really want to get to know you, Audrey."

## CHAPTER 14
*Audrey*

I was a little drunk and didn't know why I trusted this stranger. I hadn't even known him twenty-four hours, but it seemed as if we'd been connected forever. He made me laugh and listened, really listened when I spoke, even after I had guzzled two delicious, but dangerous, martinis. It had been a long time since Griff made me laugh or listened to me; for once, I felt happy, like I was a real person, not some invisible, lonely woman. And then the kiss. If Griff knew about the cradled palms and the peck on the cheek, he would...well, I don't know what he would do, but it would not be pretty. I thought of the words and image of cradled palms... my heart was racing.

Even though I had invited Logan to join me and the others, when I turned the corner toward my suite, I was relieved he hadn't followed. My brain was broken and buzzing, and I didn't know how much I could trust myself or my judgment. I found room 10-021 and swiped the key card against the electronic gizmo and the door swung wide open.

When I viewed the room, I shrieked at its size and lavishness. It was unlike the photos I had seen, much larger and much more extravagant. Its two rooms with two bathrooms exceeded my expectations of a cruise cabin. The dual walk-in closets with shelves and rods would handle all the clothing I had packed and more. Even one closet would have been sufficient. A stocked bar with a full set of glasses and dishes sat ready to use. The staff had stocked the bar with every type of alcohol imaginable, plus a large assortment of fresh fruit, cheeses, and boxes of crackers. The balcony was several times the size of the one at the Ritzy-Que, and the two chaise lounges, a table with four chairs, serving tables, and blankets made it a dream come true.

I heard a quiet knock, prayed it wasn't Logan…I couldn't remember if I told him our cabin number or not…and cautiously cracked the cabin door. Two beaming cabin stewards stood before me and introduced themselves as Alfonzo and Ruth. They moved my pair of wine bottles from the bed to the bar and set an opener beside them, before straightening the already perfectly made bed and offering to unpack our clothing when the luggage arrived. *Wow, I have never been treated like such a princess before. Our usual vacations at the Redhorn Lodge meant pinecones and mounted deer heads. This is such a switch.*

*\*\*\**

The ship had already departed Fort Lauderdale, and I knew Griff and the others would be waiting for me in a bar, but I didn't know where it was. I looked at the venue list and found eight, four on the current deck, three on the sky deck, and one near the showroom. I tried the current deck first and walked through two bars before entering the Rising Tide Lounge, where Griff and our new friends had stemmed glasses sitting in front of them. A small combo played music from the 60s and a few full-figured couples were already cutting loose, belly to belly, on the dance floor.

"Where have you been, Audrey? Did we get a new room? Where did they put us?" Griff asked. "Why were you gone such a long time?"

"I grabbed the only one available, and it's a two-room cabin."

"You're rooming with the captain?" Steve asked.

"No, Steve, they have a two-room cabin, a suite not the captain," Carlee corrected him speaking slowly and loudly.

I was still a little drunk, but somehow got my brain marching in step with my mouth and continued, "*Whatever it takes*, you insisted. I dropped the wine off, and our suite has two sizeable rooms plus an oversized balcony, lavish beyond my expectations. It was more expensive, but you said *whatever it takes.* We are on the tenth floor in 10-021, and you won't believe what our cabin looks like: two twelve-by-twelve rooms, two bathrooms, and two walk-in closets plus a full kitchen with a full-sized refrigerator and microwave. But I'm not cooking, Griff; so, you shouldn't get your hopes up that I will. One bathroom has a shower and the other has a whirl-pool tub and bathrobes and towels, all fluffy and nice, waiting for us. The bar is crammed with snacks and bottles of alcohol, but they might charge extra for those. Huge bouquets of fresh flowers decorate each room and we have an enormous balcony. Never in my wildest dreams did I imagine we would have this. I had your key card punched for a lanyard to wear around your neck."

"Woohoohoo," Gus sang out, "Now that's upscale. A suite. Two rooms. Two baths and two closets. It must have set you back a pretty pack of pennies. If you don't mind my asking, how much did it cost, Audrey?"

"I don't know, I didn't ask. They told me more money and since Griff insisted *whatever it takes,* I told them to put it on the credit card. I walked around the ship a few times, dizzy at our sudden extravagance, looking for whales, and working toward my 10,000-step goal. I didn't see any whales but finished my steps. What have you all been doing?"

Griff chugged his beer and said, "We are going to check out our new digs." He began to croon a few words of Bob Dylan's *Lay Lady Lay* while flirting with his eyebrows. "We will meet you for dinner in about an hour. Where is the dining room?"

Carlee said, "We have a table for six in the main dining room for the early seating, so let's meet here in half an hour for a drink, and we can all walk to dinner together."

"Good idea," Griff said squeezing my shoulders, "Audrey wants to test out the menu for a martini. What do you say, Hon?"

*A third martini? Just what I need.*

## CHAPTER 15
### *Audrey*

It was the first full day of the cruise, and I was excited to explore everything, find everything, and do everything. I scrutinized the daily activity menu from start to finish, circling all of the must-dos. Most of labels made sense, such as FOGA yoga class (Feeling Old, Getting Agile) geared to those with *sunny dispositions but arthritic knees*. Or the Buying Bubbly class to help *differentiate wines and champagnes, the good, the great, and the can't-live-without*. Or the Sand of My Pearl class, explaining the *various types of pearls available for purchase at the one-day-only-pearl-sale*, making me wonder how many one-day-only-sales they would have. But the activity catching my eye was the *Sail More* class, which offered a preview of all the ports where *The Broadwater* cruise line sailed. I knew I would need an armory full of ammunition to keep Griff's new-found spontaneity in full force, and it was never too early to start.

"I want to take the *Sail More* class," I told our newfound friends at breakfast. "It starts this morning in the showroom, and the cruise director is going to outline other available cruises. Griff has never been excited about cruises, so I've never investigated where all they go, but so far I'm sold, and he's not complaining, so that's a plus for me."

Phyllis agreed, "We've been on many cruises, but we're in a rut, and it sounds fun. We seem to gravitate toward the Caribbean or to the Mexican Riviera but haven't branched out to view the rest of the world. I want to add more charms to my bracelet." She raised her arm and jangled it for all to see and hear.

"What are you talking about?" Gus answered. "We cruised to Hawaii last year and have been to Asia. This cruise goes to Europe, so where else do you want to go?"

"That's just it, Gus, I don't know where else I want to go." Phyllis explained, "We should be adventurous and flexible."

Gus and Griff shook their heads, and Gus disagreed, "I'm not going to waste my time sitting in a class. I'm going to the hot tub where I can relax and watch for babes."

Phyllis quipped, "We are on a geezer cruise, Gus, you won't find any babes under sixty on this ship."

"I'm fifty-nine," Carlee piped up.

"My mistake, no babes under fifty-nine," Phyllis laughed.

I felt sure that Gus' image of a *babe* was the incomparable Sophia Loren. I looked around the room, unable to locate anyone who would resemble his idea of a *babe*. No Sophias or Marilyns or Raquels in the entire place. Plenty of women sat in the Rising Tide, both alone and with others, but only a handful were younger than I. I could tell that, like me, they had led lives of service and sacrifice, and that many were on a trip of a lifetime, attempting to fulfill past dreams. Although dressed in fashionable cruise clothes, smiling and laughing, and enjoying themselves and their friends, I doubted that they saw themselves as babes. And, I am betting, neither did Gus.

## CHAPTER 16
### *Jack Black*

The showroom could seat over a thousand people, but only a fraction attended the *Sail More* seminar. Griff had mentioned the blind man with the service dog, and I noticed them in the front row. The service dog wore a vest and harness and lurched into point position as I approached, whacking his tail against his master. I sat down, introduced myself, and asked about the dog. "What's his name, and what breed is he?"

"I call him Jack, because my name's Mel Black and I thought Black and Jack would make a good team. He's a mix of a black Lab and pointer. He likes to point, snapping to position without warning, so keep your eyes peeled in case his tail smacks erect. I've tried to train him to point to bars and pretty women, but he hasn't quite mastered the bar part, just pretty women. He stood and whacked me with his tail when you sat down, so I assume you are a pretty woman. He's a good dog and will let you pet him, if you want. Jack, please meet Audrey, but don't whack her," he joked.

I laughed and reached down to pet Jack, and he returned the favor by licking my toes making me jerk away. *Gross*, I thought, *I don't like my toes being touched.* "My husband and I don't have a dog right now, but we've usually had at least one because we've mostly lived on a farm. He's had a few Labs, but never a pointer. Griff, my husband, would probably take to Jack because he hunts and fishes," I explained.

"I used to hunt and fish, too, but I'm not quite sure what I'm aiming at these days and can't tell the difference between a sucker and a

49

trout. Jack's not trained to hunt but the pointing thing is inherent and unstoppable. I have some sight, but I trained him to watch for things that might be hard for me to see, like a dead fish on the deck or a twenty-footer, which I define as a person who might look good at twenty feet, but not so much up close. Not that that matters much to a blind fellow," Mel laughed.

"I don't know much about service dogs and how they're used. Can dogs be trained for other things, such as hearing assistance?" I asked thinking of Steve and his hearing issues. "I have a friend who could use Jack's ability, but he struggles with hearing, not sight."

"Dogs can be trained for lots of things besides sight," Mel replied, adding, "the ultimate talent would be chasing off husbands or exes, but no one has figured how to do it yet. Give it time."

Phyllis joined me just as the cruise director took the stage to begin his discussion of other cruises, ports, and excursions. I glanced around the room and saw Logan sitting two rows behind. He smiled and winked at me.

## CHAPTER 17
*Audrey*

The day passed quickly, and we agreed to meet at the Rising Tide bar, which seemed to be our watering hole of choice, at least for the time being. Gus and Phyllis were waiting for us when Griff and I arrived. Phyllis had retied her hair into a more manageable ponytail and lodged a book under her arm. Gus was nursing a beer.

"I hope you're drinking Coors, Gus. That means money in my pocket," Griff said.

Griff ordered wine for me and a Coors for himself, and the server left a small bowl of snacks to munch on, the ship's version of trail mix.

"I can't wait for dinner," Gus announced, "I've never met a cruise meal I couldn't resist. I checked the menu on the marquee and tonight's offering includes steak, shrimp, prime rib, snapper, and lamb. Of course, you can go vegetarian, but that's a waste of money, if you ask me. I'm going with prime rib. There's nothing better."

Carlee arrived next and slid a chair next to Griff. She had changed into a red miniskirt and a snug sleeveless sweater with sequins and stretched her long slender legs out in front of her. At fifty-nine she had a shapely body and used it to draw attention to herself. Her wrinkles aged her hands, face, and neck, but her legs and figure could compete with any twenty-something. She greeted the group and said, "Steve's coming down in a few. He feels embarrassed because he can't hear anything, so if you can speak more loudly, it would help. He's quite deaf, it runs in his family."

Griff asked, "So what have you and Steve done today, Carlee?"

"We just spent time acclimating ourselves to the ship, but other than that, I drank a glass of wine, started reading a novel, checked out tonight's menu, and drank more wine. I planned to lie out on the deck, but it's too cloudy for that. I should have brought more wine on board. Two bottles definitely will not do the trick," Carlee complained.

I watched her left-hand stray to Griff's right arm, but he pulled it away. He looked at me giving a half shrug with his eyebrows.

"I want to hear more about your suite," Gus asked. "How posh is it, Audrey? Phyllis and I have peeked into the rooms, but never stayed in one. This is our eighth cruise, and we thought they might give us a free upgrade, but it hasn't happened. The only way we could ever afford one is if they would give it to us for free."

I was eager to tell of the suite but didn't want to elaborate. I hadn't known any of them long enough to know if they would be jealous and so I downplayed it. "It's spacious and lovely, much better than our room at the Ritzy-Que."

"I heard if you have a suite, you get free drinks in the Platinum Lounge. Is that true?" Carlee interrupted.

She caught me off guard as I hadn't told Griff about the Platinum Lounge amenity. I had implied to the hostess Katrin that Logan was my husband and doubted they would allow two husbands. I needed it to remain a secret between Katrin and me. I wasn't sure about Logan, with luck maybe I'd never see him again.

"Where's the Platinum Lounge?" Griff asked. "We should ask about it, Audrey. It would save us money."

"The clerk didn't tell me that when I rented it," I fibbed. "If drinks were free, we wouldn't be paying for these." I gestured toward the drinks Griff and I cradled in our hands.

"Do you want to dance," Carlee asked Griff. "This music is inviting, and Steve's not here. You don't mind, do you, Audrey?" Carlee stood and entwined Griff's fingers in hers leading him to the dance floor.

*Apparently not*, I thought to myself as I watched them leave the table and fall into dance position. I looked past the dance floor and immediately spied Logan, who was seated at the bar. He returned my gaze with a smile and brought his hand to his eyebrow in a mock salute. Uh, oh. Something told me I might see him again.

# CHAPTER 18
## *Audrey*

Our table lay centered in the massive dining room. With three-thousand guests aboard *The Broadwater*, the dining room quickly crowded with people pouring into the room in groups of four or six or more. Half of the guests dined at the early seating and half two hours later. The larger tables sat toward the center of the room and the smaller tables sat near the windows. Waiters clad in white dinner jackets and black pants scurried around their tables akin to squirrels seeking acorns for winter storage. The wine stewards wore red dinner jackets with metal *tastevins* dangling from chains around their necks.

The maître d seated us, and the server and his assistant introduced themselves as Indio from the Philippines and Adie from Thailand. Giuseppe from Italy was the wine steward. Carlee insisted sitting *boy, girl, boy, girl, boy, girl*, placing herself between Steve and Griff.

Indio had just explained the evening's offerings when Logan passed by. I ducked my head in an effort to become invisible, faked a cough, and pulled the napkin over my mouth, but he paused and patted me on the shoulder, greeting me anyway. "Hello, Audrey, it's nice to see you again," he commented. He left his hand on my shoulder, but I didn't know what to say or do.

"Who the hell are you?" Griff roared. "Wait a minute, you're the dude who bought Audrey a drink at the Ritzy-Que, aren't you? What the hell was that about?"

"Yes, I did, and it would be my pleasure to treat you and your friends to tonight's wine, if you will allow me," Logan answered. He had not moved his hand yet.

"That would be lovely, why don't you join us?" Carlee piped up. "Are you dining alone, or do you have friends waiting for you?" She had emptied her wine glass and wanted to refill it.

"No, I'm all alone, in fact, I'm single," Logan answered. "I'd welcome the company. It's generous of you to include me."

He finally removed his hand from my shoulder. I feared Logan would think joining us a grand idea, but I was thinking just the opposite. It would undoubtedly be a disaster, and I hoped he would sit next to Carlee. Indio placed a chair between me and Gus, so I scooted my chair toward Griff and Gus maneuvered his chair toward Phyllis to make room. Adie, the assistant waiter, located an extra place setting, positioned a napkin on Logan's lap, and offered him a menu. "If you have questions, Sir, please ask."

Giuseppe arrived and began to distribute drink menus, but Logan waved him off and said to the group, "Let me order wine for us." He looked at the waiter, "Please bring three bottles of wine, a Cabernet, a Chardonnay and something else, surprise us. I want Australian wine, medium priced." He looked at the group, "Everybody okay with that?"

Phyllis fingered her charm bracelet, "I adore Australian wine. Thank you, Mr...."

"Hall, I'm Logan Hall from Huckleberry, Oregon. I'm a physician, a podiatrist."

Steve said, "You're a Christian Scientist? Like Tom Cruise?"

Carlee leaned toward Steve and murmured, "No, Steve, he is a podiatrist, not a Christian Scientist, and Tom Cruise is into Scientology, you know, L. Ron Hubbard, not a Christian Scientist," Carlee corrected him. "Dr. Hall is a podiatrist, a foot doctor."

"Foot doctor?" Griff replied to Logan, "Do you know anything about bunions? I have a doozy." I was mortified.

# CHAPTER 19
## *Audrey*

Griff debated what he wanted for dinner and finally Indio suggested he order both the prime rib and the snapper, but smaller portions of each. I requested shrimp creole. Carlee and Steve both opted for a small cut of prime rib, well done. Gus ordered the prime rib, "R times three," he announced, "red, raw, and rare with a baked potato, loaded, of course," while Phyllis selected a chef's salad with extra salad dressing on the side. Logan asked for the lamb kabob with extra vegetables.

The wine arrived, and Logan sampled the red, a cabernet, "Perfect," he told the wine steward. "Audrey, you drink chardonnay, would you do the honor?"

Griff guffawed, "She doesn't know anything about wine. It all tastes the same to her if it's white."

Logan ignored him and handed me a sample, "Who wants to volunteer their taste buds for the mystery wine?"

"I will," Carlee quickly volunteered. "What kind is it?"

"It's a pinot noir, an excellent choice," Giuseppe confirmed as he filled the glasses and vanished.

Logan offered a toast, "I want to offer a toast to all the feet making this trip possible."

Steve laughed, "Ditto, to all the teeth that allowed Carlee and me to come."

Not to be left out, Griff said, "Don't forget soybeans and hops. Vegetarians and beer drinkers, they're my buyers."

"And kids," Phyllis added, giggling, "don't forget about all those school kids. They're important, too. And Audrey, shouldn't we toast the alcoholics? They were your market."

I objected, "No, that wouldn't be right. They've come too far."

Everyone laughed at Phyllis' funny toast, but Logan agreed with me, "We'll leave out the alcoholics, they're probably covered in the school kids category anyway. Here, here," Logan said, holding his glass high.

The meals arrived, and Indio and Adie presented them with flair, as if a Picasso, vibrant and varied, coming to life. Gus' thick slab of prime rib seeped juice onto his plate and the liquid trickled into the potato that oozed steam and drops of sour cream and butter. Phyllis' salad spilled off the plate as Adie added the thick dressing. Logan sampled the lamb kabobs, surprised to see them swimming in heavy sauce. He pushed them aside, opting instead for his vegetables. Carlee and Steve's prime ribs were slightly smaller than Gus' and seared on the outside but bursting with juices. Griff couldn't decide which entrée to eat first, and alternated tastes of snapper and prime. "I've never caught a snapper, but I've caught lots of trout and bass. Maybe when we get to Lisbon, I should try my hand at deep sea fishing. What do you think, Audrey? Shall we go fishing?"

Fishing was always on Griff's agenda, but I couldn't envision it on mine, so I changed the subject, "Did you see the mountains of luggage the crew loaded onto the ship? Three thousand people with two or three suitcases each."

Griff agreed, "Yeah, I saw it, there was a whole shit-pot of luggage."

I elbowed him and whispered, "Griff. Watch your language, you're not in the barn."

Griff spun his head to look around and said, "Well, shit, Audrey, I guess I'm not," guffawing at his comment.

Steve continued the conversation about loading the luggage, "While I waited on deck for the hotel to bring my hearing aids, I got a glimpse of the crew loading the luggage. The process of moving all those suitcases and duffels amazed me, but what astounded me was the Depends parade. They loaded at least twenty-five cases of Depends, all with the ship's ID tags attached, meaning they were for individuals, not for the ship to sell. How many people do you imagine wear adult diapers on this ship?"

"I doubt they'd bring them if they didn't use them," I answered. "If they need them, they need them, it all depends."

"*Friends*? The cast of *Friends*? They are here? Is Joey here?" Steve said craning his neck to look for the actor.

Carlee responded brusquely, "Audrey didn't say Friends. She was still talking about Depends."

Phyllis laughed, "The joke's on you. Security X-rays suitcases but don't bother with Depends' boxes for obvious reasons, and they work great for smuggling liquor or wine bottles aboard. Four to six bottles can easily fit in one box. At the end of the cruise, people either dump the boxes or break them down, put them in their suitcases, and take them back home for the next cruise. Easy."

Steve stood up and pointed, "I think I see him. The tall guy with the lavender shirt. Look, Carlee."

Carlee rolled her eyes and drained her glass, "Oh, my, this is going to be a long cruise."

## CHAPTER 20
### *Audrey*

"What an amazing meal and now to the bar!" Griff declared as we left the dining room.

"Which one?" Gus asked. "This ship has at least six, and we should try them all out. We could do a pub crawl because we don't have to drive."

I was more interested in seeing the show than doing the pub crawl and said, "That might be overkill. Why don't we walk the dinner off, Griff? A nice romantic walk around the ship. And I noticed that the entertainment is some singers and dancers. We should check it out."

Griff was slightly limping and said, "No, let's just go to the bar. My bunion hurts, and I'm too tired to walk."

"Yes, Audrey, I saw they are offering a Vegas type show with lots of singers and dancers, but it doesn't start for another hour, allowing plenty of time for a little drinky-poo. Let's try a bar on the Sky Deck," Carlee suggested. "Come on, Steve."

"You go ahead without me because I can't hear diddly and won't enjoy it. I'm going to the casino where you don't have to hear anything. In fact, not hearing the constant chiming of the machines will make the casino far more interesting," Steve told her. "And if I'm playing, they'll serve me free drinks, watered down, but free."

I interjected, "Okay, Griff, let's go to the Sky Deck. I walked around today but didn't make it to the top deck. While I was waiting to get our new cabin, a few people talked about a bar on the twelfth deck called the Night Sky. The sun will be setting soon, and it's supposed to have a great view with pink, blue, and orange reflections, a big light show. I can finish my step count up there."

The group, less Steve, entered into the elevator, but it didn't go to the twelfth floor, rather stopped at the eleventh, necessitating a walk up one flight to the highest deck.

When the elevator stopped, everyone except Logan exited. "I've changed my mind," he said. "I was in one of the smaller bars yesterday, and I struck up a conversation with a lovely lady. I'm going to go back to see if she happens to have returned. I'll meet you before the show." Logan gave a slow deliberate smile at me before turning toward the stairs.

Carlee and I led the group while Phyllis, Griff, and Gus followed; I noticed Gus was panting by the time we arrived at the bar.

The Night Sky Bar, a cozy, open-air bar, seated four or five dozen people with a small dance floor at its core. A table near the bar was piled high with plaid blankets to ward off a chill. A CD played music from the sixties, but a sign told us the Night Sky Trio would be playing later. Darkness had fallen, and the stars shined brightly, twinkling high overhead.

I was in awe of the white waves contrasting the black sea with the stars twinkling above. The warm breeze announced that we weren't in Idaho anymore. "Isn't this beautiful?" I said to Phyllis and Carlee. "With all the lights in Hunter and other cities, I had forgotten how amazing starlight is. Griff will love this."

Griff and Gus had paused on the staircase, "You need a little more exercise," Griff told Gus as they finally reached the top of the stairs. "You ought to try what I do, you know, dancing in the sheets a few times a day, un-fossilizing yourself. Audrey loves it, and I'll bet Phyllis would, too. She seems like the type who is always up for a good time. And she's a pretty one."

Gus agreed, panting, "This cane slows me down, Phyllis makes me bring it, but I don't really need it. Yeah, she's pretty, all right, but you should have seen her in college. She turned all the boys' heads, and it took years for Phyllis to say yes to my continued proposals. She carries around a few extra pounds, but she's the same Phyllis, and nothing bothers her, not a bit. Don't worry, she and I get plenty of lovin', it's quality lovin', not quantity though. By the way, who's the foot doctor guy who is paying attention to your wife? Do you know him?"

As they made their way to the top step, Griff responded, "No, I don't know him, but some foot doctor is the least of my worries. Audrey can take care of herself. She won't put up with any foolishness."

I heard Griff's comment, but when he turned and looked toward me, I saw him wink at Carlee. *Why was he winking at Carlee?*

I tapped him on the shoulder, "Griff, I'm going to get a sweater from our room and take a walk around the ship. All this wind is making me chilly, but I will be back in a few minutes. Don't order me anything yet because I want to walk off the dinner and wine we had."

Once again Griff ignored my presence. Was he interested in Carlee? I should have felt jealous, and would have years ago, but today I found a new emotion beginning to overwhelm me: indifference. I hurried down the two flights of steps and disappeared into our suite to freshen up a bit. I threw on the sky-blue cashmere sweater I had bought myself at Christmas, dabbed on some pink lipstick and brushed my wind-blown hair. Then I did a once over of myself in the mirror. I thought I looked fine but speculated whether I could pass for sixty, seven years younger than my age. I walked three doors down to the Platinum Lounge and asked Katrin, "Has my husband arrived yet?"

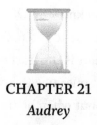

## CHAPTER 21
### *Audrey*

The Platinum Lounge had emptied as guests departed for dinner or a show or the casino or wherever. Logan had already initialed Griff Lyon on the sign-in sheet and sat alone on the love seat while savoring a glass of red wine. He hadn't spoken directly to me about the lounge earlier, but I certainly interpreted his meaning, or what I hoped he meant.

When I saw him, my wonka came alive again, and I smiled, maybe even grinned. "I hope your hint about going to a different bar was an invitation for me to join you." Awkward emotions, as tangled as a bird's nest, surfaced, and I thought maybe I should just throw myself off the ship now, eliminate the whole middleman thing of Griff finding out and keelhauling me. A scary thought entered my confused brain: *What if I were wrong and Logan was waiting for someone else?*

Logan stood as I approached him and nestled my hand in both of his exclaiming, "Wow! Audrey! You look beautiful. I'm happy you came, but truthfully, a little surprised. I mean, I hoped you would... I'm just so glad you are here."

My awkwardness had elevated like an airplane ejection seat, and I started again with the stammering. "Uh...yes...yes, I've been married a long time, over four years, I mean forty-eight years, lots of rocking and rolling. Griff, too, I mean Griff and I were married, not just me," I said, not responding to what he said, but rather to my guilt about being married and my unfamiliar emotions that kept popping up in odd places making my innards squirm.

Logan began to laugh and a twinkle in his eye launched me into a blushing, blithering idiot, "Yes, well, forty-eight years. That's a long time."

After settling down a bit and gathering my senses, "I just wanted to tell you, because Griff said this was my trip, something I've dreamed about, but it surprised the heck out of me. He said it was all about being spontaneous. So, when you hinted that you wanted me to join you, I thought *why not?* After all, I can't be spontaneous after the opportunity vanishes, can I?"

Logan continued to massage my hand and smiled, "I would agree with that. And, Audrey, I do enjoy you, talking to you and seeing you, but I might have come on too strong, and if so, I apologize, but if not, I'll keep trying until you throw me to the sharks."

My face cooled down, and I was growing braver by the minute, but my leeriness had not disappeared completely. We both ordered and sipped our wine, and I stopped chattering, relieved at the pause in our conversation. I looked around at the room, desperate to see something else to talk about, other than Griff and our half-century together.

We sat silent for a few minutes, and I decided to turn another direction, "I wonder if this ship carries ice cream, which is one of my passions," I asked, wondering where it might lead.

Logan nodded his head, "Yes, that's a good idea. Let's finish our drinks, and we can go to the ice cream shop. There's one on the main deck."

## CHAPTER 22
### *Carlee*

The Night Sky Trio, made up of one Latin and two Asian musicians, entertained the guests with an expansive variety of American songs, although the musicians struggled with English, as Griff learned when he tried to request a song. Carlee wanted to hear *Margaritaville*, and the trio played a version of it, even though the words seemed a little off.

Carlee had nearly finished her third glass of wine since dinner, and without Steve to temper her, Griff thought it likely she would have three more. She had passed the stage of drippy and moved into sloshy with slurred words and a teetering gait. Well into middle age, she used her figure and sway to turn men's heads, but alcohol and sun had taken their toll on her leathery face, wrinkled neck, and purple-spotted hands. However, when she drank alcohol, her keen wit and her mischievous personality came full circle. Phyllis appreciated banter as much as anybody but thought Carlee's devilish chatter ran a little risqué. Both Griff and Gus seemed amused and maybe even charmed by it.

"Just out of curiosity, do you boys still have the love juices flowing? I mean, we are all retro, that's what my kids call me, and I guess retro means old and shriveled, like prunes or raisins. They don't know my love juices work fine, bubbling to the surface particularly when I meet handsome men like you two," she ran her hand slowly from her boobs to her tubes asking, "How about you, Phyl, do you enjoy the old sugar stick?"

Carlee had been jabbering sexual innuendos non-stop for nearly thirty minutes, stirring chuckles among the three and people at nearby tables,

64

but the *sugar stick* comment cranked Griff and Gus into hysteria, and they laughed to the point of near hyperventilation. Phyllis, not to be left out, giggled and fanned herself feigning hot flashes. "Oh, Carlee, you're making me blush. I love studs, just not misspelled studs, like STDs, so I stick with my Gussy Poo."

Carlee chuckled and stood and took Griff's hand, "Let's dance again, Griff, we were just starting to get it going." She rose and wiggled her ass but was a little shaky and needed to support herself with Griff's arm, "Come on, Honey, Audrey won't care, neither will Steve. Steve's at the casino, and Audrey hasn't returned from getting her sweater. I can't imagine what she is actually up to. Let's do it." She wiggled her eyebrows and winked at Phyllis.

Carlee's comment troubled Griff, but he didn't interpret her comment to include Logan. He looked the room over, wondering where Audrey was, he was sure she was fine, walking per usual. Or reading about Mrs. Robinson in *The Graduate*. He set his drink on the table and guided her to the dance floor. Carlee was unsteady but followed his lead, and within seconds they were wiggling and jiggling to the Night Sky Trio's version of *Proud Mary*.

Carlee collapsed in her chair at the song's end and emptied her wine glass as Steve walked into the bar. "Come on, Carlee, let's go back to our cabin. I won about twenty bucks, and we should celebrate. Nobody ever wins anything in cruise ship casinos, and twenty dollars is damn good," Steve bragged.

"Does the casino pay out in U.S. dollars or ship money?" Griff asked.

Steve misheard Griff's comment, "Shit money, you mean money laundering? They don't launder money on the ship, although they are registered in Grand Cayman. They don't give you real money though, just shipboard credit to be used in the shops or bars. Let's go back to our room, Carlee, you look tired, and I can't barely hear the music anyway. It's been a long day." He took Carlee by the arm and guided her toward the stairs.

"I've always loved to dance, but I am nearly worn out," Griff sighed, as the trio began another song. "I wonder where Audrey went. I know she wants to go to the show tonight. While we are waiting for her, Phyllis and Gus, you should shake a little leg, too, it's good for your health."

"No, not me," Gus stated shaking his cane, "Walking up the stairs nearly did me in. I don't want to have a heart attack out on the dance floor. Phyllis would keelhaul me, or worse."

"How about you, Phyllis, would you like to dance? Do you prefer slow or fast? I have enough oomph to do one or two more, but after *Proud Mary*, I could do with a slow dance," Griff suggested.

"I wouldn't mind, but I'm with you on the slow dance. Let's see what they play and pick one we like. If we sync, then like a young bride, I'll move into position," she agreed, grinning.

An Asian/Latin version of Johnny Mathis' *Chances Are* came on, and Griff gathered her hand into his and led her to the dance floor, "You're a great dancer, Phyllis. You are easy to talk to and fun to be with," he murmured squeezing her closer than she intended. He twirled her around, moving his back toward Gus and nipped her ear with his lips. Startled, she jerked back, looked at him, before burrowing closer. She was taller than Audrey and when he drew her close, her head nestled below his chin. He liked it. She did, too.

She whispered, "I do lots of things well, you might be surprised."

# CHAPTER 23
## *Phyllis*

While Phyllis and Griff were wrapped around each other dancing, her heart pounded, and her lower forty intensified, making her fidget with eager anticipation. Gus found no joy in dancing, so Phyllis' dance card sat empty regularly, but through the years she had danced with many others, and she had never been quite as aroused as she was now. She knew what was happening and had no intention of stopping it or slowing it down. Forty years of sex with Gus had been mostly wonderful, but menopause had introduced frost bite to her southern wasteland. Gus had the desire, but not the design, and sex between them became rarer and rarer. She had discovered adventurous ways of compensating, but now, Griff stirred her in a way she hadn't felt in a long time. She and Gus were happily married, so why were her semi-dormant sex mechanisms suddenly shifting into high gear?

Griff had been a one-woman guy. Audrey was good enough for him, maybe not perfect, especially in the night-time department, but he never considered straying. She took good care of him, and that's all he needed, but variety was the spice of life, and it might be nice to see who else was out there, just for the fun of it.

Griff also detected a rhythm, and not just from the in-harmonious Night Sky Trio. His lower parts were also primed. He was puzzled because he hadn't used the blue pill, and these days, he couldn't pull the rabbit out of the hat except by ingesting the magic potion. *Chances Are* was winding down, and Griff wondered what his chances were and decided to take a chance. He whispered to Phyllis that he was going to look for Audrey and invited Phyllis to accompany him.

"Are you sure?" Phyllis asked, hoping that it meant time alone with Griff. "I'm dying to see your suite, but what about Audrey? She might be resting, and I wouldn't want to disturb her." Thinking on it further and not wanting to miss out on this opportunity, she quickly added, "The show starts pretty soon, so maybe we could check it out right now. I know Audrey was looking forward to tonight's performance, so she's probably already be in the auditorium."

Phyllis accepted his offer eagerly and told Gus, "Gus, Darling, Griff invited me to look at their suite. I'm sure you aren't interested, but I am, so I'm going with him. We'll meet you in the auditorium. Try to get a seat toward the middle on the left-hand side, and we'll be there in a jiff. You and I are just poor teachers, and I want to see how rich folks live. Save us six seats because the auditorium will fill up. The show should be starting shortly."

Gus agreed and took the elevator to the main deck where the auditorium was rapidly filling up, while Griff and Phyllis walked the two flights to Griff and Audrey's suite.

On the way to his suite, Griff wrapped his arm around Phyllis, and his hand inched south to her derrière, quickening her enhanced libido, but when they approached the Platinum, he moved his hand upward to her back and replied, "I don't know where Audrey is, she's been gone a while. She wanted a sweater, but I hope she didn't fall in the ocean."

Phyllis thought, *I hope she didn't fall in the ocean either, but I wouldn't mind her staying lost for a little while,* but said, "Don't worry. She can't fall into the ocean, and we haven't had a tsunami to wash her overboard. She's probably walking off dinner."

"Look at this, the Platinum, a private bar," Griff pointed out. "It's pretty swanky. It must be nice to be rich enough to have your own private club." He looked in and noted a couple people playing cards and drinking wine, "Lucky guys."

"I'm excited to see your suite, Griff. As I mentioned earlier, I've peeked into suites but have never gone into one. I hope I'm not being forward," Phyllis said.

"It's pretty flashy, I have to say. Audrey did a good job of talking the desk clerk into giving it to us," Griff answered, wondering if Audrey would be in the suite when they arrived.

He worked the key card to open the door to their suite calling out, "Audrey, are you okay?" He closed and double locked the door before checking the bathrooms and bedroom. Everything was neat and tidy with no Audrey to be seen.

Phyllis passed through the sitting room onto the deck to view the black sky and black water and white wake from the ship. This deck was twice the size of hers and contained lounge chairs topped by woolen blankets and a small table with a bottle of wine and glasses awaiting them. Griff approached her from behind and wrapped his arms around her, placing his hands on her ample breasts, and kissed the back of her neck, "I've been wanting to do this all night. You are a lovely woman. Beautiful, funny, and exciting."

She shivered at his touch and turned in his arms and kissed him back. She noted her Mrs. part had moved from tingling to throbbing and thought, *I hope I don't go from throbbing to thrusting to damn fast. He's a sexy beast and I'm ready. Oh, dear God.*

# CHAPTER 24
*Audrey, Griff*

Our marriage had been hectic, yet wholesome, until we retired. We had clicked through the community obligations like clockwork, conforming to the mores of our community: military service (check). Church involvement (check). Boy Scout leadership (check). PTA, (check). Solid community-based careers, farming for Griff and nursing for me (check). I served on the library board and helped with church events. Griff represented local farmers at the soybean commission. We had paid our dues and served the community appropriately and acceptably.

Our two boys, Jeff and Mike, both born after Vietnam, were now forty-five and forty-eight, educated and married, and had given us four grandchildren, three girls and a boy, all of whom were now in middle school. They both lived in a western Oregon town named Huckleberry, a few miles west of Portland, but made regular trips to Hunter to visit us and give me my much-desired *grandma time*.

Through the years, hard work and dedication created prosperity for our family. As a young farmer, Griff wanted and needed help on the farm, but didn't want to pay for it. He depended on our sons to help, even while prepubescents. Griff never considered my nursing position a real job because I worked in a chemical dependency center, *not a real hospital with sick people*. And since I worked only part-time, he expected me to help on the farm, especially caring for the animals, milking the cows, and tending the chickens, as well as my traditional roles of mother, cook, laundress, and housekeeper. Between my job, the animals, community obligations, and the boys, most days my energy level hovered between inert and empty. Sex became sporadic, and eventually both of us became drained and disinterested.

Griff worked hard at farming, taking little time off for vacations and relaxation, which always involved hunting or fishing. I talked to him about trying new and different things when he retired, but he had other ideas and narrowed rather than expanded his interests. He began restricting his activities to those he knew, namely fishing, hunting, and sex.

The newly retired Griff found time to watch TV and discovered several channels he had not watched previously: the X-rated sex channels. They aroused his libido, but his ability to perform sex floundered. He blamed me for his lack of sexual prowess, saying that my sexual appetite had never been a smorgasbord but since menopause, it had waned and resembled more of a continental breakfast buffet with lukewarm coffee offered at roadside motels. His words were both true and untrue. I was interested but didn't focus on sex as my only goal in life. Unlike Griff. His lack of sexual prowess was not an issue with me, but it embarrassed and frustrated him. He acquired a new vocabulary to tint his language with interesting and funny comments, but often he overdid it, compensating for what he lacked in the bedroom. I drew the line when he referred to my breasts as *his kettledrums*; it was the bridge too far.

He noted with interest the television advertisements for ED problems, and one day, he left without telling me where he was going, but I, sneaky person that I am, always check credit card receipts. He had traveled to a different town where he could buy a little help without being recognized, after all, he told me, he wasn't old, and ED only happened with old men. *Tell that to the hunks who are modeling the ED supplements,* I thought to myself. He visited fifteen drug stores and came home with fifteen different packages, each promising a new and improved sex life for him and his partner, meaning me. The photos on the packages suggested the drugs would also transform his looks to a younger and more virile Griff. He also bought me roses and a Costco-size supply of female lubricant. Did he imagine that was going to spur my interest? When I looked at the gallon sized bottles, I was stunned and frightened. Had he lost his ever-loving mind?

The ED supplements mostly proved to be useless, although combining both pills and creams sometimes helped. After a few weeks, we received a notice about the *Welcome to Medicare* program requiring completion of its annual questionnaire about all kinds of things, including libido. He had known for a long time his sex drive was not what it had been as a young man but figured his gray-hair and his shriveling and shrinking body parts were connected. His doctor disagreed and assured him he had a little blue pill that would return the jingle to his jingle-berries and wrote the prescription.

Griff wolfed down his first pill on his way home from the pharmacy. Apparently, they gave him the fast-acting type because the moment it reached his bloodstream, *things* started to happen. He swept me into our bedroom on the way into the house and began disrobing both of us. He asked what I had done to myself saying I looked different, having blossomed into a beautiful woman with considerable sex appeal, even though he had left me only an hour earlier. I looked in the mirror, noted my still-drab hair, no make-up, and my new Walmart sweats, wondering if the doctor had given him the wrong medicine. Griff's obsession with the results of the pill led to using it three times a day. The pill bottle read *as needed,* and he told me he needed to fondle my breasts and body morning, noon, and night. Pre-blue pill, he had complained my breasts were small, barely big enough to even touch, but now, he thought them robust and healthy, screaming for his attention. His life was good, mine was different.

## CHAPTER 25
### *Audrey*

I fell in love with Griff from the first moment I laid eyes on him. We had met at a dance during my freshman year of college, but he was three years older and ready to graduate and join the Navy. He had studied agri-economics. I dreamed of living in France and earned my degree in French, minoring in European studies. But once we married and moved away from school, those dreams predictably vanished. It wasn't as if Hunter had many jobs requiring a degree in French, so I re-enrolled in a local community college to find a useful career and went into nursing, obtaining licensure as an LPN. I convinced myself that France could wait, as I had found the man of my girlish dreams—smart, handsome, hard-working, and he loved me. Without question, he loved me.

Growing up and later in college, I wanted my own career, to earn my own money, and be my own person. I never sought recognition, but if and when I received it, I wanted it to be mine, not Griff's.

My mother, in her wisdom, advised me to remember the word *enough*. She advised me to remain independent *enough* to assure that if I wanted to walk away from a situation or relationship, I could, because I would have *enough*: *enough* education, *enough* money, and *enough* confidence to be strong and powerful, if I needed it. I never forgot my mother's sage advice that had gained salience in recent years as I considered, more than once, if I had had *enough* of Griff and needed to walk away. But I stayed.

As a young wife and mother, I was optimistic, trying to be cheerful although this was not the life I had anticipated for myself. I loved life

73

and Griff and our boys, and later, our grandchildren. My friends called me a firecracker, the first to try something new, go someplace new, and do something silly. I loved being involved with people and groups, and worked hard to maintain all my relationships, although we lived in the proverbial middle of nowhere.

In my opinion, Griff had not retired well. Through the years we had talked about what we would do once we finished working. Our bucket list was long: traveling, advocating for causes we cared about, exercising, attending concerts, plays, and events, learning new languages, and trying new things. I'd throw out an idea and he would agree, sometimes enthusiastically. As it turned out, obviously, the bucket list had been mine, not Griff's, and when we retired, the bucket list split into two, his and mine.

I knew we were moving in different directions but didn't quite know how to stop it. Griff had no interest in a single thing on my list, so I was caught off guard when he surprised me with this cruise. I agreed to it quickly, hoping he had returned to the adventurous, fun-loving Griff I had known back in the day. Through the years, we had been frugal and saved money to build our portfolio, plus we were fortunate to sell the farm for far more than we ever expected. We didn't need to worry about money, but old routines are hard to break. This trip was extravagant, especially now, flying first class and opting for a suite instead of a less expensive sea-level, bare basics room. The higher cost might raise his hackles. *Whatever it takes* was not Griff, but I would take him at his word.

And now, I had encountered Logan who had a zest for life that Griff had lost many years ago, maybe fifty. Continually concerned about money, Griff's work consumed him, but we didn't realize the impact it made on the other side of life: play. Over the decades, we hadn't done much of that at all.

I knew people who had taken cruises, found new friends, and had even fallen in love, but that wasn't my style. I had vowed to *love, honor, cherish,* and *obey,* and while I abandoned the *obey* part within weeks of our wedding, I had adhered to the rest and had planned to keep my vows until *death do us part*. I just didn't know when that would be, and I didn't want to kill him. But as Griff had become unreasonable, I sometimes found myself rethinking things. And now that I had met a man who had taken a genuine interest in me, I find I am doing it again. Rethinking. I liked Logan and the attention he paid me, but he had come on so quickly. So many things to think about. Was he really a podiatrist? Was he really a widower with no wife or did he have a wife waiting in the wings, wanting to blackmail me or even kill me? My mind zigzagged all over the place.

When I was with Logan, my interior juices boiled and bubbled, making my lower deck hot and fizzy, and I wondered if he felt the same, and if so, what I should do about it. Griff would have told me plain and simple, *I have a hard-on, Honey, time to do the dirty*. I knew he loved me, but the sex thing had gotten out of control and all his romantic inclinations had vanished. On the other hand, Logan certainly was romancing me and had not mentioned sex, but what about the sex thing? Maybe it was time to find out who I had had enough of: Griff or Logan?

## CHAPTER 26
### *Gus*

Showtime approached quickly, and Gus had his hands full trying to shoo people out of the five unfilled seats. Phyllis, Griff, and Gus had departed the Night Sky bar together, but they also went their separate ways and now he wondered where everybody had gone. He knew where Steve and Carlee were; she was either sobering up or getting drunker, one of the two, for sure, and Steve probably was bemoaning his lost listening devices, as well he should. Inability to hear would make things difficult for the entire cruise. Gus, too, wore hearing aids and disliked them, but he wanted to participate in the conversations around him, rather than guessing at conversations and being wrong half the time.

Phyllis considered herself open to everything, but thought Griff a bit crass, especially when he talked to and about Audrey and their sex lives, case in point, how he mentioned *doing the dirty* with Audrey. TMI, her students had called it. Too much information. Griff crowed about everything, including ranking each bump and grind on a scale of one to ten.

With her quick wit, Phyllis seldom crossed the line to risqué, but her friends enjoyed her self-deprecating, bland-as-bananas humor. Gus had been surprised when she agreed to go off with Griff especially after Carlee's comment about the *sugar stick.*

Gus craned his neck looking for Phyllis or any of their friends, when Logan tapped Gus on the shoulder, "Room for me? The auditorium has filled, and it looks as if these are no-shows. Where are all your friends?"

"Oh, hello, Logan. Please sit down and join us, uh, I mean me. I don't know what the delay is. I know where Steve and Carlee are because she was loaded, and Steve suggested they go to their cabin. Audrey, Griff, and Phyllis? I don't know why they aren't here yet. Phyllis and Griff went to his cabin, so he could show her what a suite looked like. Audrey wanted a sweater, but she left a while ago. Phyllis must be on her way here, and I imagine Audrey and Griff have hit the sheets working on part two of their three-a-days. He sometimes calls it parring her course. He's got a euphemism for everything."

"Did Phyllis get lost? She wanted to see the show too, didn't she?" Logan asked.

"Yes, she probably got lost and is wandering around the ship. I figure she'll find the showroom at some point, but I don't know if she'll be able to locate us in the dark. This room holds 1,000 people, and it's packed. Plus, the three-minute warning light already flashed."

\*\*\*

I had just walked through the door when Gus looked over his shoulder and waved me over. The auditorium darkened as I sat down between the two men and the show began. Lights, camera, action.

Two seconds later Logan picked up my left hand. Apparently, my show was just beginning.

## CHAPTER 27
### *Phyllis*

Phyllis didn't resist when Griff nudged her into the bedroom. She was playfully horny and figured he was, too. She hadn't been this aroused for years and the sensations created a type of shock and awe. Menopause had delivered drought, discomfort, and disinterest in anything sexual and abstaining, except for a handful of dalliances, hadn't been difficult for her. Gus was interested but he hadn't sexually stirred her in a long time. Their sex life had gone from spiking the football to a dull game of Go Fish.

When Griff and Phyllis tumbled over each other into the bed, she laughed, but quickly changed her mind, "Griff, I'm scared. I want this, but you're married, and I am, too, and Audrey might barge in at any time. We can't do this," Phyllis halfheartedly pleaded with a half laugh, half moan.

"Don't worry about Audrey, she'll be watching the show, and we'll make the second act. I'm horny and clearly you are, too. Let's do it and see where it leads," he fondled her oversized breasts with his hands and added, "lovely, just lovely."

"What if I get pregnant?" she giggled aloud adding, "just kidding, menopause fixed that."

"That's a good one," Griff chuckled, "because I'm fresh out of condoms, except for the one in my wallet, purchased in 1965."

Griff undid his belt and began unzipping his pants when she placed her hand over his, thinking she could deter him but instead noted he was rising in her hand. He exclaimed, "Oh, my God, I forgot to use my blue kazoo."

"Kazoo? You play a kazoo? Why would you need a kazoo?" Phyllis puzzled aloud.

"Not a kazoo, I sometimes call my magic blue pill that, the one I use to do the dirty, but maybe I don't need it with you because I'm ready to rumble," caressing her ample breasts and midriff.

Her eyes opened wide as she jerked back and blurted out, "No, stop, you have to stop."

"Why? What's wrong? Did I do something wrong?"

"Yes… no, it's not that. It's just…wrinkles. I have wrinkles. Lots and lots and I'm geriatric, inflexible, and fat. I don't want you to see me."

Griff rearranged her clothing and began to kiss her, starting with her navel and moving north to her neck and ears, finally kissing her hard using his tongue, murmuring, "I don't care, and no, Phyllis, you are vintage and classic, to be honored and respected, and I want you."

She didn't know if he was serious or not, but his words ignited her and suddenly, she didn't know how, her muumuu spilled to the floor. and they both were naked.

"I don't know if I'm coming or going." She closed her eyes, inhaled, and moaned aloud, "Actually, I do know," she thought noticing the increased moisture in her foo-foo.

They didn't need foreplay; they were all over each other, and she thought of nothing except his being inside her. When they finished, he was panting and sighed, "Oh, my God, Phyllis, that was wonderful. I don't know why you see yourself as old and inflexible. You are amazing, supple, and responsive, and we scored an easy touchdown." Her charm bracelet jangled against the pillows.

## CHAPTER 28
### *Audrey*

The intermission lights flickered on, but I couldn't recount a single moment of the singers and dancers in Act I. Logan had caressed my left hand non-stop, occasionally lifting it to his lips and kissing it one finger at a time. His hand was soft, yet firm, and I liked it.

Logan dropped my hand as the lights blinked on and people began to stir, heading toward the restrooms or bar, to return to their cabins, or watch the ocean waves. I stood and rubbed my hands together, alternatively patting them on my skirt trying to restore my circulation from his clutch. I smiled at Logan and replied casually, "Intermission. I'll see if I can find Griff."

Gus asked, "And Phyllis. Could you watch for her, too? I'm going to hit the restroom. Logan, could you hold our seats? Hopefully, everyone will be here for the second act."

The auditorium had been filled at the start of the revue, but now scattered groups of seats sat idle. First full day on the ship, full bellies, and a couple drinks meant the auditorium population dwindled. With the average age of the cruise guests over seventy, many options were available for post-dinner entertainment, including bars, restaurants, the casino, library, or watching the ocean from a balcony. Sleeping was another option, appealing to the more elderly, travelworn guests.

I pivoted my head around the showroom looking for Griff and Phyllis but didn't see them and turned to go a different direction, but Phyllis noticed me, waved, and called out, "Woo-hoo, Audrey, we're over here."

On the upper level, toward the back sat Griff and Phyllis, whose hair had once again ceded to the wind and stood at attention. Her lipstick was smeared, and her mascara smudged across her cheek.

Griff stood and asked, "Where have you been, Audrey? We've been looking for you."

I charged up the steps and beelined it to where they were seated, "We're on the lower level, way down front. Down there," I pointed to where Logan stood peering at the crowd. He gave a little wave.

"What about Gus?" Phyllis asked. "Did he get lost? I don't see him." She stood and craned her neck over the shifting crowd.

"Gus saved our seats, and I sat by him for Act I. Carlee and Steve didn't show up, and I didn't know where you were, Griff. Logan joined us because he couldn't find another seat. After the first act, Gus went to the restroom, and I came to find you. Logan is holding our seats." I added, "Oh, look, Gus is back, and Logan is headed out, probably to the restroom. You know old guys and their prostates. Why don't you two join Gus and Logan, and I'll hit the ladies' room myself before Act II?" The three-minute warning light flashed, and I murmured, "I'll be right back."

Griff helped Phyllis descend the steps, and they joined Gus in the plush seats he had saved. I lagged behind, wondering about Phyllis' lipstick, mascara, and uncombed hair. *No, they wouldn't have,* I thought. *No way.*

I wondered for the umpteenth time: *Had I had enough?*

Logan was leaving the men's room when I spied him, and he reached for my hand and whispered, "Audrey, would you prefer watching the rest of the show or joining me for conversation and a drink at the Platinum?"

"Is there any place I would rather be?" I answered in a whisper while he caressed my hand. "Next stop: Platinum Lounge."

## CHAPTER 29
### *Audrey*

Although the Platinum was a cozy bistro/bar with limited food and drink and only able to serve half a dozen people at a time, apparently another guest was hosting a party meaning it was crammed when Logan and I arrived. We asked Katrin for a glass of wine and exited quickly.

"Our suite lies three doors down from here," I pointed out. "Why don't we step across the hall to our cabin? We have a couple comfortable chairs and plenty of room for entertaining. Since Griff's at the show, he'll be tied up for at least an hour. We can spend uninterrupted time getting to know each other, if you are willing."

We entered the suite and looked around. "My goodness, what happened?" I asked. "It's a mess. Griff must have taken a nap because the bed looks like it's been slept in. He likes order, and I would never have left it this way because he'd be livid."

I started to straighten the bed, but Logan caught my hand, drew me toward him and kissed me. I opened my eyes and started to pull away but didn't. My mind raced through a thousand words describing him and my current emotions.

He was sexy; how could I resist? He was kind and such a gentleman, I had liked it when he held my hand, but now, yikes, he was again heating me from the inside out. I loved Griff, had always loved him, and felt fortunate that we meshed for all these years, well most of them anyway. The last three seemed as though we were on divergent paths. I hadn't been in the mood for Griff's affection for several years and didn't know why exactly, but I knew the hot water in my spigot had grown cool. Logan's touch left me warm and fuzzy inside and out. I thought, *maybe I am just horny after all these years.*

Logan double locked the door before he started back-walking me toward the disarrayed bed. I resisted, sort of, but he didn't give up until I twisted away from him.

"I have to make the bed," I announced firmly.

Logan countered, "We can freshen the bed later, let's take advantage of the show that's going on downstairs and create our own showtime right here, right now. You have turned my legs and feet to jelly, Audrey, and I haven't been this aroused since Joan died. Just being with you has lit a fire in my libido, and I'm having hot flashes and a hard-on at the same time. And I have to tell you, this is not me. Not me at all."

I shuffled to the sofa and began chattering, but my words came out wrong again, "Not you? It's not Griff either. Griff's married, and I just met me. I can't kiss this, and I need to go to bed, I mean I need to go. Go someplace else."

Logan laughed, "You make me happy when your brain forgets to work, Audrey, it's so refreshing." He knelt beside me and slid my sandals from my feet. "Easy, Audrey, slow and easy." He began caressing my toes, as he had my hands earlier, one toe at a time. My eyes turned to goggles as he began to suck my littlest toe. I tried to stand, but the toes on my right foot were occupied, and the left foot was evidently stuck to the floor. My mind flashed to Jack the dog that had slobbered on my toes earlier today. I forced that thought out of my head, and Logan continued going north, kissing my knees and thighs and continuing toward my face, slow and soft.

In my entire life, no one had ever played with my toes, and I hadn't kissed anybody except Griff since we had married. But my body had turned to concrete not allowing me to move. I wanted to kiss Logan more than anything but seemed to be nailed in place, glued to the floor. I finally touched his face and held it between my palms ready to give in to my emotions and kiss him, but I still couldn't move, and guilt pounded on my brain. But my brain started working again, and it rationalized, *It isn't actually a simple kiss, rather a complex finale of all my senses: seeing, smelling, feeling, tasting, and hearing. God, I haven't felt this alive in years. Good God, I'm overanalyzing; just kiss him.*

As I began to pucker, the doorknob jangled, and someone pounded on the door. Griff called, "Audrey! Audrey! Are you there? My key card won't open the door."

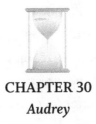

## CHAPTER 30
### Audrey

I was horrified but my previously concrete legs now moved fine, and I morphed into a whirling dervish. I became a teenager again, caught with my pants down. They weren't down, yet, but they would have been if Griff hadn't interrupted.

"I'm in the shower," I called through the door to Griff. "Let me throw on a robe on. I'll be there in a sec."

Logan started toward the bathroom. "No," I hissed, "the balcony. Griff has an enlarged prostate, and it doesn't work very well. He'll have to pee for sure. Hide out there while I divert him. When we're gone, you can sneak out the front door." I gave Logan a gentle shove toward the balcony. "There, hide out there, and don't come back in until we leave. Five minutes."

Floor to ceiling glass windows displayed every inch of the open balcony with no place to hide. A locked, metal barrier fenced off the entrance to suites on either side of us. Logan covered himself with one of the blankets and plastered his frame against the wall, hoping it would shield him, but quickly realized it was akin to being an ostrich. He poked his head around the barrier and saw no one in the darkened suite next door, so he crawled over the railing and inched around the barrier, all the while dangling over the deep Atlantic Ocean for a few seconds. In the process, he dropped the blanket, and it floated down into the water. Immediately, an earsplitting alarm screamed, and a bright spotlight flashed to where Logan stood. A voice boomed over a loudspeaker for all to hear, "Man overboard. Man overboard."

I learned later that Logan had streaked through the neighbor's dark suite to the hall, tripped over suitcases still sitting in the middle of the floor, and landed on his butt. He feared he would see Griff, but thankfully Griff had already entered our suite.

I heard the *man overboard* call, as well as lots of yelling by people in the hall, so I threw my robe over my clothes and glanced in the mirror, noting my hair jutting out in nine directions. I quickly jammed my head under the faucet for enough water to feign having taken a shower. I moved about the room imitating a hyperkinetic maniac, checking for anything awry, then opened the cabin door and panted, "Sorry, Griff, my stomach was churning, maybe I was seasick, and I wanted to relax, so I skipped the performance to take a long shower. How was the show?"

The siren blared, and the light continued to shine at the balcony next door when Griff raced out to our balcony. "What the heck is going on? Man overboard? Someone must have jumped from the next room. They'll never find him in this dark." He peeked around the barrier, and downward into the ocean. The spotlight targeted the blanket adrift with the waves. "Damn, some dude took a dive. He's gone for sure."

I shadowed Griff to the balcony, looking around, wondering where Logan went. I thought he had climbed over the rail. But had he jumped or fallen into the ocean? Was he the man overboard? No, that couldn't be. Tears began to flow down my cheeks. Griff pointed to the blanket being washed to the bottom of the ocean by the waves.

"Did you see anybody? Hear anything?" Griff was talking to me, but I was barely able to answer, and just shook my head.

"No, nothing," I quivered, in a painfully thin voice. I didn't know if he could even hear me. Had Logan fallen into the ocean? I raced to the hallway just in time to see what I thought was Logan's backside as he turned a corner...or was it? There were so many people in the hallway, I couldn't be sure.

## CHAPTER 31
### *Audrey*

The following morning brought rain, wind, and dark clouds to a turbulent sea. Everyone on board, crew included, resembled the weeble-wobble figures of the seventies, trying to keep their heads up and their breakfasts down on the high-crested sea. The rain had soaked the walkways and the giant splashes made it risky to walk on the teak deck.

Griff and I went to breakfast early. We both had trouble sleeping and the raging weather didn't help. I was distraught at the thought of Logan's demise, still trying to hold back tears, but Griff was eager to spread the news about the *man overboard* episode. It seemed unfathomable that my new friend had plunged into the ocean. Carlee and Steve joined us before we had finished our coffee. The tables were arranged for six, and Griff and I sat across from each other.

Carlee and Steve both wore seasickness patches behind their ears and were bright and cheery, even though they teetered and had to grab the backs of chairs and tables to maintain their balance. They took their seats at the opposite end of the rectangular table from Griff and me. Carlee nursed a Bloody Mary, decorated with celery, shrimp, and parsley. Steve held a handful of pills that landed on the floor when the ship pitched from one side to the other. He knelt down to gather them up, but the ship rocked again, and he sprawled over the floor, pills askew.

Griff and Carlee stood and offered Steve a hand up, and I inched around the table to regather the pills.

"Eleven, there should be eleven pills," Carlee said to me." I looked around and finally found nine, but the tenth and eleventh were nowhere to be seen.

"I only see nine," I had lined them up in front of Steve, counting nine. He looked them over and told me, "It's the little white one that's missing, for my blood pressure. And a green capsule, but I don't remember what it's for. They have to be here on the floor."

The three of us lowered ourselves to our hands and knees, searching for the evasive pills. Two servers saw us and joined in the search and two more helpful guests made seven searchers.

"Here's a pill," one of the waiters shouted, holding up a small green capsule. "Is this yours?"

"Yes, that's one," Steve cried.

Griff exclaimed, "Here it is, I found it," and held up a tiny, pale-yellow pill.

"No, that's not his, it's white," Carlee sighed. "Steve's blood pressure pill is white and round. Are you sure you brought it, Steve? Or did you leave it in our room?"

Steve looked the pills over and stood and pushed his hand into his pants pocket and pulled out a small white pill, "Here it is, I put it in my pocket, I forgot. I'm so sorry."

Griff started to stand, but the ship pitched again, and I steadied him before standing myself and assisting him to his feet. Carlee thanked everyone, and the helpful guests and staff scattered, leaving us alone.

Carlee asked me, "Did you see the show last night? We went to bed early, you know, Steve's seventy-eight and all this lounging by the pool wears him out. Hopefully, they will have a repeat performance at a two o'clock matinee for us oldies before we dock in Lisbon, so we can see it."

Griff wanted to relate the tale of the man who was now in Davey Jones locker, "Now that we solved the pill mystery, did you hear about the man who jumped off the ship last night? He was in the cabin next to us. We didn't see it, but we saw something in the water directly below our cabin, maybe his body. In a flash the ship stopped, and the emergency boats splashed down into the sea. It just took a few seconds, and the crew was all over it."

"We didn't hear anything about it. When did it happen?" Carlee asked. "Did he jump or fall?"

Griff continued, "We're not sure, Audrey was in our cabin, and the siren went off, along with lights and staff running around. I had just returned from the show, but Audrey didn't see anything either. She was a little seasick. We had never met the people next door."

"Hi, Phyllis, Gus," Griff greeted, pulling out the chair next to him where Phyllis was aiming her ample body. "The ocean is throwing a temper tantrum today; you can sit down by me. It's easy to get tossed around when the sea is this angry. Would you two like coffee?" He rose to go to the coffee station, but the server came by with a coffee pot and water pitcher, filling all our cups.

Gus, seated next to me, suddenly rose and explained, "I'm topsy-turvy because I don't have my sea legs yet. Between the ten-foot swells and the raging wind blowing across the deck, my stomach is churning. Phyllis is much better than I am at staying upright and avoiding seasickness. Excuse me though, I'm going to lie down to rest. I'll run by the ship's store when they open to get a motion sickness patch."

The group watched Gus as he departed, and Phyllis announced, "Don't worry, it's only the storm. This happens nearly every cruise. He'll be better tomorrow. I'm going to get a ham and cheese omelet and bacon. Would anyone else like to join me?"

I said, "We must be in the edge of a hurricane. I swallowed a seasick pill, but I might get a patch like everyone else seems to have. Do I need to get them from the ship's doctor, or can I get them at the ship's store?"

"You can buy them from the ship's store that opens at ten," Logan murmured from behind, touching her shoulder, "or you can ask this doctor for a sample that I carry in my little black bag. They work well, and I have extras."

I was bewildered, but my relief was tangible. "Logan!? I thought you…I mean, I, uh, we didn't see you last night, and I wondered if something had happened to you."

Logan sat down where Gus had been seated a few minutes before and looked around the group. "I hope you don't mind if I join you. How is everybody this glorious morning? Being on the ocean during a storm excites me, even though the rough seas indicate the sea is incensed about something. Everybody knows the adage *the calm before the storm*, but the reverse is also true, *the storm before the calm.* Sunny, serene days and smooth sailing lie straight ahead." I thought Logan sounded chipper, as if nothing had happened the previous night.

"Yes, where did you disappear to last night, Logan?" Phyllis asked. "I hoped you would join us, but you never came back. Did you go to bed early?"

Logan smiled, "Sort of, I encountered an old friend, you might say a FWB, and we reacquainted ourselves. Nothing's better than old friends." He smiled at each person individually, pausing at me, but besides Logan, only Phyllis knew the meaning of FWB and had to explain it to all of us. Her students, in their school chatter, had explained that it meant *Friends with Benefits,* and usually the benefit was casual sex. I wondered what friend and what benefits Logan found last night.

## CHAPTER 32
### *Audrey*

The storm lasted throughout the morning, but by noon the seas calmed, and the sun finally made its appearance. It turned bright and warm, and people began moving toward one of the four hot tubs or three swimming pools. The deck had dried, and walking was no longer a hazard. The lounge chairs abutting the pool filled up and the outdoor bars buzzed with customers.

When Griff and I arrived at poolside, Carlee had already claimed several lounge chairs for the group and positioned herself on one with a margarita and a book. She wore a pink and chocolate colored bikini and looked stunning. With no time to shop for clothes before going on this trip, I wore a navy-blue one-piece purchased a few years earlier, but it still fit, and hadn't faded. Griff had told me to bring a bikini, but he must have been thinking of our trip in the early seventies because I hadn't had a bikini in a long time. Griff wore his only bathing suit, orange flowered, vintage 1970s. Slathered in sunscreen, zinc oxide covering his nose, and a baseball cap reading I ♡ Soybeans, he looked exactly like a soybean farmer from Idaho. He held a half-eaten hot dog in one hand and a beer in the other. All he needed was his hunting rifle to complete the picture.

Logan arrived a few minutes later and seated himself next to Carlee. "Did you save this one for me?" he asked.

"You're sitting in it, so I guess it's yours. Is this your first cruise, Logan?" she asked.

He responded, "Oh, Lord, no, my wife Joan and I cruised through the Panama Canal from California to Guatemala several times to work with Doctors without Borders. Lots of people had foot issues, mostly from lack of shoes and infrequent bathing, but we also saw people with serious issues, like club feet that had never received either surgery or manipulation to correct them. I worked with surgeons to improve the injuries, but often the bones and muscles had adapted to their misshapen feet making it tough or even impossible to correct. We usually sent kids to the U.S. for surgery. I treated every type of foot disease known to mankind while in Guatemala. But we also took a few pleasure cruises through the Mediterranean. How about you and Steve?"

"Steve retired ten years ago from his dentistry practice, and we have taken a cruise every year. His ex-wife takes a good share of his income, so we don't sail more often than that. Between the two of us, we have eight kids, and they can be an issue. His kids believe I married him for his money, and my kids hope I married him for his money, but they are all wrong," she laughed. "I usually say I married him to avoid dentist bills for my five kids and eight grandkids. But the truth is, he's a kindhearted and gentle man, and we get along well. He's my third husband and the best of the three."

Logan chuckled, "You gotta respect those doctors. They'll do anything to keep you in their clutches."

"Anyone want to join me in the hot tub?" Carlee invited as she slid off her lounge chair. "It's empty now but will fill up when people realize how warm it is."

"Sure, I will," Griff answered, "Audrey rubbed nearly a whole bottle of sunscreen on me. She loves massaging me because it turns her on, but I wouldn't mind getting some of it off." He winked at Carlee who laughed.

I shifted seats to where Carlee had been seated and now sat next to Logan. I asked quietly, "What happened last night? I thought you fell into the ocean."

He whispered, "No, but the ship police chased me after I crawled across the rail to the other patio. I dropped the blanket, and they thought I had jumped. The spotlight was bright, but I doubt they knew who I was or took a picture. I'm still lying low, though."

"I was worried you died. Did you get hurt?" I asked him.

"My arthritic knees stopped working midway over the rail, and I crashed to the floor of the patio, but luckily, I fell onto the patio, not the other side otherwise I would have gotten quite soggy, and I wasn't in the mood for a swim," Logan kidded. "I tripped over some suitcases when I was trying to exit and ripped the knees of my pants. I was afraid Griff would still be in the hall, but instead I met a barrage of crew members, including the medical team, not to mention about a hundred guests who were headed back to their rooms after the show had finished. Between all the people and the siren, I'm sure I looked frazzled, but no one commented."

I let out a giggle, "It serves you right for trying to seduce my toes. By the way, who is your FWB?" I innocently inquired although I suspected that I was his FWB.

He confirmed it with a whisper, "You, silly girl. I met up with you. You are my Friend with Benefits. You have so many benefits I can't count them all. You are amazing, I loved last night, but want more, and want to meet up with my FWB again today. By the way, did you buy your seasick patch yet? If not, and I don't see one behind your ear, we can go to my cabin to get one, and I will apply it. I'll trade you the patch for another FWB meetup. Even-Steven. My cabin is less elegant but less risky than yours because Griff doesn't have a key. How about it?"

I was still trying to recover from the thought of him being overboard, and here he was trying, once again, to get me in the sack. What is it with men, anyway? Can't we just be friends? I remember Sally and Harry having a similar discussion in *When Harry Met Sally* so maybe it was an age-old question.

I turned my gaze to the hot tub and saw Carlee cozying up to Griff, both with drinks in their hands. He was laughing, and she was sitting close with her arm draped across his shoulder. He didn't seem to be in any rush to remove it. "Okay, it's perfect timing, but I want to go to the ice cream stand, instead of going to your cabin. I don't want to encourage your toe-sucking fantasy because it might lead to something more dangerous," I said, rising and tossing towels over the six now-vacant chairs to hold them for later.

"I can only dream," Logan sighed, shaking his head, "You don't know what you're missing, Audrey."

"That's what I'm afraid of," I laughed.

He teased, "There is something to be said about toe sucking, and you have ten lovely toes to tempt me. But, at any rate, we need to retrieve the seasickness patch from my cabin, not the ice cream parlor, but if you are refusing me, I'll get the patch, you get the sorbet, and we can meet up in a few. It's your loss, though."

## CHAPTER 33
### *Griff*

Seeing she was getting nowhere with Griff, Carlee left the hot tub to the boys. Griff and Gus relaxed in there with Coronas, basking in the effervescence and energy of the bubbles flowing in and around their bodies. Steve decided to forgo the hot tub and sit with Phyllis. He, too, draped himself with towels.

Gus sighed, "Aah, we are living the good life. These bubbles tickle and torment my magic wand as well as the twin whirligigs that get lonesome these days. I wish Phyllis would tickle my twins like these bubbles do. Getting old is not for the weak willied."

Griff nodded his head in agreement thinking, *Phyllis certainly had no problem tickling my twins.*

For the sixth or seventh time, Griff read the hot tub's list of warnings for using the hot tub. Pregnancy and children under five were no-no's, but not problems for him and Audrey. Medications and alcohol were no-no's, but he did take medications and was drinking a beer, and probably would have a second. Griff only had a couple prescriptions for thyroid and arthritis but, surely, they wouldn't count. The blue pill might count, though, and he'd ask his doctor at his next visit. He looked at Gus, whose BMI must be approaching forty, and wondered about his health. He decided to ask.

"Gus, did you read the sign about medications and alcohol? We're both sitting here drinking alcohol and I, for one, take medications, but only a couple. Does it mean quantity of medications or the actual medications themselves?"

Gus shrugged his shoulders, "Who knows? I don't want any part of them, and don't usually take any, but Phyllis practically has a nervous breakdown about it. Every damn pill has a gazillion warnings, so I tune them out. One has a warning label saying *don't take if you are dead or near death*. Seriously? I can't count all the pills the docs have prescribed rotting in our cupboards. They give me pills for everything, but a lot of them contradict each other. I have a pill to speed up my pulse and one to slow it down. I have a pill to wake me up and another to help me sleep. I have a pain pill that says don't take if you use this other pill, both prescribed by the same doctor. I have a pill case with breakfast-lunch-dinner-bedtime alarms, but I get them mixed up. And it can be confusing. For example, what about brunch? If I skip breakfast, do I skip the pill, too. Pain pills are nothing but a pain in the butt." Gus guzzled more of his Corona before continuing.

"My heart doc told me to quit booze, but I enjoy my Scotch and don't want to quit my two or three drinks a day. I'm different from Carlee, though. She has a problem in my opinion." He looked across the deck at the other hot tub where Carlee now was nursing a lime green drink with an umbrella and fruit attached. "The doc sent me to an endocrinologist for diabetes, but she wasn't for me, and I didn't go back. Another doctor gave me a sleep study to see if I slept okay, which was a waste of time. I sleep fine, but they gave me an alien mask anyway. No way I'm gonna use it because it would be a definite sexual turn off for Phyllis. Phyllis hounds me, of course, but I don't mind because that's her job: to hound me.

"I'm supposed to have more medical tests after this cruise, but I'm not gonna take them because they'll say they are inconclusive. They'll just want me to pay for more tests. I don't remember what they're for, and that's another thing: I keep forgetting things. I lose my keys occasionally and forget I lost them. I take a pill to help my memory but most days I forget to take it. As I mentioned before, getting old ain't for the weak willied. Nor for the weak witted," Gus quipped.

"I get it," Griff agreed. "You don't realize you will become forgetful when you are thirty. Or forty…even fifty. It creeps up on you, and before you know it, you start to get air farts in your brain. The thoughts are alive and well, stashed in a wayward brain wrinkle, maybe even doing brain cartwheels, and you want to bring them out, but you can't find 'em, no matter how hard you try. It's worse than losing your keys. Then one day, without warning, they burst out, maybe even in another conversation. They call them *senior moments*, but instead they should call them *fatal air farts*, because that's what they are. FAF. Hey, Gus, how about that? I created a new acronym. But I'll probably forget it and call it FBF."

"I like it. FAF. Fatal Air Farts. You should be aware, however, FBF is already taken. Flashback Friday. When I taught school, the kids talked in acronyms, and I learned a few because I wanted to know if they were talking about me. Some students referred to me as *RR, Retro Rich*, my real name, but that's better than *GG or Geriatric Gus.*"

Griff laughed out loud. His use of social media was limited, and he didn't have any idea about the texting, or the variety of acronyms people used. He asked Gus, "What does Phyllis do for fun? She laughs all the time, a chuckle, belly laugh, or sometimes just a giggle. She seems to find humor in anything and everything. From what I can see, she definitely is a fun person, comes across shy initially but once you get her to talk, she's clever, especially with words."

Gus agreed, "Yes, she's a corker and was a popular teacher at school. The kids loved her and would do anything for her. She taught high school English and put on plays and created opportunities for kids to succeed in areas other than in schoolwork. We didn't have any kids of our own, so she adopted the whole bunch. She taught for over thirty years, and kids still drop by the house or call her. She goes on social media and keeps up with them online."

Griff sat up on the edge of the hot tub, feet dangling in the water saying, "I'm getting too warm and am ready to get out. The water must be one hundred and five degrees. It's hot. By now, Audrey has had time to warm up, so I'll go see how warm she is. She can be fiery hot, too." He laughed at his comments, stirring as he thought of Audrey. Naked.

Gus stood up to wade out of the hot tub, slipping on its smooth wet bottom and losing his balance. He had left his cane with his clothes and didn't have the extra support he would have liked. He sagged into the moving water unable to catch himself, bumped his shoulder, and his left hearing aid released from his ear. It swooshed as it exited, and his eyes immediately darted to the bottom of the turbulence trying to locate it. The hearing aid got caught in the effervescent swirling stream and swished up, down, and around avoiding Gus' grasp. He finally grabbed it and righted himself to put it back in his ear. The battery had released from its cage, and he eyed it toward the bottom of the hot tub, but it, too, was in the maelstrom. He held the hearing aid in one hand and stretched for the battery with his other, finally pinching it between his fingers.

"I have new batteries, but I gotta dry this sucker out. It isn't waterproof or even water resistant. I gotta get it dry." Gus pulled himself up the stairs and reached for a towel briskly dabbing the wet aid.

"Are you okay?" Griff asked.

"I'm okay, but the damn aid isn't. It's electronic and wet, and I'm sure it won't work. Phyllis has a hair dryer. I can try that."

"That might work, but you might try rice, dry rice, the same as when you get a cell phone wet," Griff offered. "I dropped mine in the commode one time, and Audrey put it in a plastic bag of dry rice and left it there for a few hours. It works fine now. She threw the rice away though; she didn't want to eat it."

Gus nodded, "Okay, that's a good idea. I'll try rice if the hair dryer doesn't work. But first I've gotta pee. The innards aren't the same as when I was young because I have to pee all day and half the night, too. The problem is that most of the time I can't do anything except dribble."

"I hear you, Brother," Griff responded.

Gus quickly stepped away from the hot tub and headed toward the public restrooms. Once inside, he opened the fly of his swim trunks and stood waiting for something to happen. He counted to ten, held his breath before a dribble, and a squirt came out, hardly enough to write home about. He shook himself off and began to button his fly and splash! A dinky little splash. He looked down. His hearing aid had slipped from his fingers and now sat on the bottom of the commode. *Damn, now what do I do. Don't flush.*

Instinctively, he reached down and plucked the device from the water with his fingers and shook it off. Gross. Where was Phyllis when he needed her? "Phyllis...Come here!" he shouted, as he exited the restrooms. "Phyllis!"

## CHAPTER 34
### *Gus*

While Griff and Gus had been in the hot tub Steve dozed sporadically on the deck chairs, silent because he was embarrassed about getting so many things wrong. Phyllis also faded in and out of sleep, not exactly asleep, but not awake either. Her conscious mind ruminated on the cruise and its amenities, the food, the excursions, and yesterday's rough seas. Her semi-conscious mind bobbed between Griff and Gus with intermittent thoughts of hungry sex with Griff and more anemic sex with Gus. Gus' sex drive had become a month-old carrot of late but sex with Griff had freshened and invigorated her. She loved Gus, but Griff had once again aroused her womanliness, which was welcome. She felt sexual joy with Griff, but not with Gus, making her wonder if she should follow Marie Kondo's advice? Should she say *thank you for your service* and toss him out because he no longer gave her joy? She smiled at her capricious thoughts of Gus and Griff and their diametrically opposed sexual choreographies.

When Phyllis heard Gus call her name, she jerked up from her near nap, "What the heck?" She heard him but didn't see him. Had she dreamed it?

"It's not working," he cried from behind her and sounding desperate. "My thingamabob stopped working. I dropped it in the hot tub, which is bad enough, but then I dropped it in the toilet and it's wet. Can you dry it off and fix it? Griff said it might work if I put it in a plastic bag of rice. Did you pack any rice?"

Phyllis' mind was on sexual choreography and she had no idea what thingamabob he was talking about. She jumped up and trotted over to him, "What thingamabob did you drop, your penis? How'd you drop it in the toilet? And Griff is wrong about drying it in rice because it won't help. It's your prostate, you've had prostate issues for three years. Surgery might help, but not rice." She started laughing at the preposterous thought of putting his thingamabob in a plastic container of rice.

"Not my dick, Phyllis, my hearing aid. It fell into the toilet. It's wet and it's not gonna work." Gus held out the dripping hearing aid and placed it in her hand. "Eeowee. Yuck, you dropped your hearing aid in toilet, and you thought it was ok to put it in my hand? That's gross, but we might be able to fix it. I couldn't figure out what you meant when you said your thingamabob. Take it to our cabin and dry it with the hair dryer."

"Dry my penis with the hair dryer? What good will that do?"

"No, Gus, go dry the hearing aid while I beg a cup of dry rice from the cafeteria." She used two fingers to pass it back to him, dipped her hands in the pool, hoping the chlorine would kill off anything toilet related on her hands, and wiped them on the towel.

Carlee heard Phyllis and Gus' animated chatter and dried herself off. She looked around but didn't see her husband. "Where's Steve?" she asked.

"He was lying there a couple minutes ago," Phyllis answered. "Right now, Gus' *thingamabob* is dripping, and we need to find rice, but we'll see you at dinner."

Steve reappeared with a plateful of nachos and said, "We are having rice for dinner? I like rice, but what else are we having?"

Carlee raised her eyebrows, wondering about Gus' *thingamabob*.

## CHAPTER 35
### *Audrey*

Griff had removed himself from the hot tub by the time Logan and I returned from ice cream. We had talked about a bunch of things, from our kids to our retirement aspirations.

Carlee's face tinged pink from the sun as did Griff's back. She located a sunhat in her swim bag and Griff asked me to find him a t-shirt. He glared at Logan and said, "Where did you two go? Is the cafeteria open? What's for lunch?"

I said, "Yeah, everything's open. All kinds of things, pizza, salads, and soups. Anything you want, but we had ice cream."

"We can do ice cream later, but what I want is an all-American cheeseburger," Griff stated.

"I'm not eating, but I'll have another Bloody Mary." Carlee said, "with shrimp and vegetables, it should count as a meal, right?"

"By the way, Doc, will you look at my bunion while we are getting a little sun? It seems to be growing, and it is painful when I put shoes on, even my new sandals are bothering me. Do you have any quick tricks to get rid of a bunion?" Griff asked Logan who agreed to take a look and give an opinion after we had cooked ourselves in the hot tub.

He and I watched as Griff and Carlee made their way to the Broadway Bar for their meals. Carlee had placed her hand on Griff's arm. I didn't say anything, holding in my anger as usual. My mother's *enough* conversations were once again blossoming in my mind.

"Let's get hot and wet," Logan whispered, smiling coyly.

I looked at him hesitantly and my eyes widened, "No, I don't think so. Griff is…"

"You don't like hot tubs?" he asked innocently. "Audrey, you have a dirty mind, I just meant getting in hot water."

I chastised myself, *yikes, I'm sounding more and more like the talk on the sex channels Griff fancies.*

An hour later Phyllis and Gus arrived, each carrying a heaping plate of food and a Diet Coke. They had changed clothes and now Phyllis wore a purple flowered cover-up over her bathing suit and carried a large aqua swim bag embroidered with purple dolphins on her shoulder and a Boise State ballcap almost covering her unruly hair. Gus wore black swim trunks and an orange and blue Boise State Broncos t-shirt that gapped above his trunks. He tugged on it every few seconds in an attempt to hide his protruding belly and the tufts of gray hair peeking out.

"We had to take care of Gus' hearing aids. Hopefully the blow dryer, rice, and some time in the sunshine will dry them out." Phyllis exclaimed. "Where is everybody?"

I answered, "Griff and Carlee went for sustenance. Griff: food. Carlee: Bloody Mary. Steve left again, and Logan and I are about get warmed up in the hot tub. Want to join us?"

"That sounds fun, but not until I eat because breakfast didn't stick with me. I want to save room for tonight's feast so I'm eating a salad and a couple deviled eggs," Phyllis explained. "You two can go ahead and relax in the hot tub. I'll join you in a few."

A super-sized cheeseburger lay on Gus' plate, along with French fries and a pile of nacho chips with a mound of guacamole. I thought, *that's a danged big burger*, but said, "I'm glad you are feeling better, Gus. That's a good-looking burger."

"Yes, much better. I didn't eat breakfast, and I'm gonna make up for lost time. Man, oh man, these cruise people know how to cook. I'm gonna eat this first, but I'll get to the hot tub in a few minutes, too," Gus said as he collapsed on the lounge chair. "I prefer the swimming pool over the hot tub, but the water is chilly."

Griff returned with a plateful of food identical to Gus' lunch and sat down. Gus asked, "Griff, I meant to ask you earlier, what did you think of the show last night? I thought it was okay, nothing giving me goosebumps, but acceptable. Live performances are fun. Phyllis loves them better than almost anything, don't you, Hon? How about Audrey, does she enjoy live shows?"

"Yes, last night was amazing," Phyllis added, remembering the horizontal hula she and Griff had danced in his suite last night. Her mind shouted *I didn't like the show nearly as much as I enjoyed strumming Griff's ukulele,* but she said quietly, "We missed the first part of the show but what I saw was wonderful."

## CHAPTER 36
*Audrey*

"Our health is our most important asset," I often warned Griff, whenever he objected to my yoga or jogging or any of my other physical activities. I knew I looked healthier than many other *women of a certain age*, but as I looked at my hands, I wondered how old I looked. Although my face was relatively wrinkle-free, my hands had taken on the texture of crepe paper with thin skin and a couple purple polka dots. My rings had grown too big, and I needed to resize them. Griff's hands were smooth and unwrinkled, and I wondered why men's hands didn't age as women's hands did. Although Griff called my cheeks rosy, I viewed them more as masks for the freckles that had plagued me as a youth. At any rate, on the wrinkled skin scale, the score was two and ten, face being two and hands maxing at ten.

When the boys had played football in high school, the coach required two-a-day August practices to get them in shape, occasionally adding three-a-day practices as the weather allowed and they became fit and strong by the time the football season began. Griff remembered the boys' getting strong and connected our thrice-a-day sheet-banging directly to my healthy appearance. *Cause and effect,* he said, but I thought differently. Nevertheless, he was insistent, regardless of my reluctance.

I knew Griff was fixated on the three-a-days when he bumped into me on the Sky Deck. We had only done the dirty once, and his blue-pill libido would be back in full swing. Logan and I had been walking for almost an hour, working on our 10,000 steps, but he had just peeled off to go change from his athletic gear. I was strolling, not in any particular hurry, watching the waves and the flying fish and the scattered clouds responding to the wind. I was idly taking a break from life, mostly lost to the world, except my thoughts kept returning to Logan and Griff. It was Friday, and I had met Logan only a short time ago, but it was like I had known him forever.

Griff wanted to take the elevator, but I convinced him to walk, and we descended to the main deck where a pianist played music from the 60s. We stopped at the Ocean Waves Bar where he ordered a Coors and I ordered a fancy-dancy water before moving on. We passed through the library where many people read, worked on jigsaw puzzles, played chess, and flicked squidgers in a friendly game of tiddlywinks.

We walked through the shopping area, stopping to admire the jewelry and I tried on a pair of especially elegant, and expensive earrings. *A girl can't have too many,* I thought, and I turned to Griff, "What about these? They're natural pearls from Australia."

I expected him to growl at the thought of such indulgence, but he said, "They're expensive, but they make your ears look perfect for nibbling, so let's buy them and go upstairs so I can examine them more closely. Let's play doctor." The three-a-days hadn't left his mind.

I wanted the earrings, but I wasn't in the mood for ear nibbling, "Maybe later, the ice cream store is right around the corner and it's time for my sorbet fix," I answered firmly and moved toward the stairs.

"Hey, there's Logan," Griff said by way of greeting. "Can we join you?"

"Sure, why not? I just finished a scoop of caramel ice cream, but I might want another," Logan answered, smiling. "I might even go for a sundae. Everything tastes better with whipped cream and a cherry on top."

I felt as out of place as a unicycle in a marching band and wanted to drop out of sight. I volunteered, "I'll get them, what do you two want? I'm having sorbet, maybe mango. Griff, do you want chocolate, as usual? Logan, what would you like?"

Griff answered. "Rocky Road and ask if they can make it into a sundae, whipped cream and maybe a cherry."

"That sounds delicious, I'll have the same. I love whipped cream," Logan offered.

As we nibbled our sweet treats, the conversation vacillated between feet and soybeans, and I watched a tennis-match conversation. Back and forth. Forth and back. Two separate conversations and neither listened to the other, but both trying to one-up the other. *Indeed, Griff was a soybean and hops expert, his life's work, and Logan was a foot expert.*

"Speaking of feet, Audrey," Griff said, "did you get a pedicure? Your feet and toes look great."

I withdrew my feet, desperately hoping to hide them, but it was too late. Both men leaned over to look at my toes. I had been a party to fancy footwork, all right, but not exactly in the salon.

"Pedicure, uh, no, not exactly." I looked at Logan before I looked at Griff, and realized instantly that I should change my story, "Actually I did, I wasn't going to tell you because they're expensive and you've never approved of spending money for them, but I thought why not? We seem to be spending money like we have it, so why not?"

Logan said, "You have beautiful feet, Audrey, listen to one who knows feet."

## CHAPTER 37
### Audrey

It was our third evening on the ship with an Italian dinner theme showcasing an array of pastas and sauces. Cheese plates sat on every table with unrecognizable condiments. Griff refused to try those condiments, but asked Indio for ketchup and mayo and they appeared immediately.

All seven of us chatted and laughed, when suddenly, seemingly out of breath, Gus paled, pushed, his entrée away, and scooted his chair back. "Is something wrong, Mr. Gus?" asked Adie from over his shoulder. "Does the pasta not taste good? Would you prefer something else?"

I was seated next to Phyllis who gasped, "Are you all right, Gus, Darling? You're not eating your dinner. The lasagna looks fantastic all drippy with cheese. Aren't you hungry, Hon?"

"I'm a little dizzy and need to lie down for a while. If they can put this in a doggie bag, I'll eat it later. Excuse me, folks." He rose and left the table leaving his cane on the back of his chair. My nurse's training kicked in, and I started to stand and go with him, but Phyllis patted my hand and shook her head.

"I'll join you in a few, Hon," Phyllis called after him, taking another bite of lasagna. "Could you box this up for Gus," Phyllis asked Adie. "I'm sure he'll finish it later."

Logan said, "Let me know if he's not okay, and I'll check him out. I carry my stethoscope and would be glad to give him the once over. I specialize in feet, but I can do other body parts, too." Logan sat across the table from me and cast a subtly flirtatious smile in my direction.

108

"That's generous of you, Logan. We might take you up on your offer because the ship's doctors are expensive, and they don't accept insurance. I slipped at the pool last year and sprained my ankle and ended up on crutches for the remainder of the cruise. X-rays. Medicine. Physical therapy. Wheelchair and walker rental, crutches. That little fall set us back about $3,000. And our insurance dissed it because we were in Costa Rica," Phyllis remembered.

"I don't have an X-ray machine, medicine, or PT, just my handy-dandy stethoscope and a little expertise," Logan replied, "but I'm glad to help if I can."

Steve said, "You know, Doc, you're a podiatrist and I'm a dentist, but what I need is an audiologist. I can't hear anything. What's wrong with Gus?"

"He said he didn't feel well, but didn't mention why," Carlee explained to Steve in a louder than usual voice. "He's sick."

Several minutes later the maître d appeared at the table and placed his hand on Phyllis' shoulder. "Miss Phyllis, you need to come with us," he whispered, assisting her in moving her chair from the table.

Phyllis gave a little shriek, and pushed her chair out from the table, almost knocking Indio down in the process, saying, "What's going on? Tell me now."

I again started to rise, but this time Griff grasped my arm. I pulled away from him and followed.

The maître d clasped Phyllis' elbow and escorted her to the lobby where a large crowd had gathered waiting for the second seating. They parted like the Red Sea when we stormed through, leaving a six-foot wide swath to the staircase. Logan abandoned his meal and followed us, but the rest of the group stayed behind. Near the stairs a smaller crowd had assembled, including a ship's officer, nurse, two response team members, a stretcher, and Gus, who lay sprawled over the top two stairs.

"Gus, darling, are you okay? Did you fall?" When he didn't answer, Phyllis looked at each member of the medical team in turn. "What's wrong with him? Is he dead?"

"No, Ma'am, he fell and smacked his head, knocking him out for a few seconds, and now he is a little groggy, but he's alive. We're moving him to the infirmary and will put in an IV and perform a couple tests. Check his heart and lungs. You can't do anything right now, and you should finish your dinner and come down to deck two in half an hour."

Logan advised, "Phyllis, you should do what they suggest. You and Audrey should finish your dinner, and I'll follow the team to the clinic to make sure they treat him well. I'll be back in a few minutes."

Phyllis and I returned to our table to finish our dinner and report Gus' condition to the rest of the group. Teary mascara ran down Phyllis' face and she gasped for air, attempting to suppress the sporadic sobs her throat emitted. Indio came by to inquire about dessert. We all had finished our meals and refused anything sweet, but Phyllis said, "I'm worried, and need to calm down. Gus is my honey bunch, and I need chocolate, please. Could I have a hot fudge sundae, double chocolate, double whipped cream, but no maraschino cherry? It's the only thing I know to calm me," she said, adding, "And a diet coke."

## CHAPTER 38
### *Audrey*

Phyllis and I followed the signs and arrows through the warren-like configuration of hallways and doors leading to the medical clinic. Located deep within the ship, a line of several people waited to see the doctor, but the LPN spied us and ushered us through several more doors, even farther into the bowels of the ship, where we found Gus and Logan in a tiny room dwarfed by a variety of complex-looking machines, all pale green. Gus was apparently asleep because he didn't open his eyes, and Logan stood quietly beside him, stethoscope draped around his neck.

"What's going on?" I asked Logan, "What happened?"

"The symptoms all point to a heart attack, but the doctor is still running a few tests," Logan replied solemnly. "Does Gus have any heart medicine?"

Phyllis cried, "Heart attack? Oh, no. Heart medicine? No, he has bottles and bottles of pills, but most days he refuses to take them. He says he doesn't need them because they don't work anyway. He's supposed to have a Medicare checkup annually, but he says he's healthy and refuses to go. At his last physical, the doctor told him to give up drinking, but it didn't go over well. He has a couple drinks a day, usually before bed. He coached football and regularly exercised, but since he retired, he doesn't do much. How long will he have to stay in the clinic?" She babbled, her eyes dripped tears, and her face was blotchy, "He's my everything, and he can't have had a heart attack."

Logan said, "Heart's not my specialty, but Dr. Lewis, the ship's doctor, recommends Gus remain in the clinic for a few days to rest. They do the tests on board the ship and fax the data to a specialty doctor in Miami who interprets it. This ship's doctor and the Miami doctor will consult and decide what would be best."

"Where's the ship's doctor? I want to see him," Phyllis demanded.

"Him is a her," Logan answered. "The ship's doctor is Dr. Vivian Lewis, lovely woman, and I'm sure she's a good doctor. Her diploma from Harvard Medical School is hanging on the wall." He pointed to the diploma.

"Oh, gawd, a woman doctor," Phyllis moaned. "Gus will have a cow. He hates doctors and thinks women doctors aren't good for anything except delivering babies. This will never do. We need a different doctor."

Logan offered, "I'll talk to Gus when he wakes up. The women doctors with whom I have worked are bright and capable. They are podiatrists, like me, but still, a doctor is a doctor."

Phyllis continued, "How about you, Logan, you're a doctor. Can't you help him? He would probably respond to you," She gave a nervous laugh.

"Heart attacks aren't in my range of expertise. Now, if he had a wart or a bunion or a devilish case of athlete's foot, I'm the guy," Logan reassured her, patting her on the hand.

Griff, Steve, and Carlee inched into the tiny room, now crammed with six visitors and as many machines, "I have a bunion, but so far, you haven't done diddly squat," Griff pointed out to Logan from the doorway, adding, "You keep pussyfooting around," which brought a smile to Logan's face.

Dr. Lewis squeezed into the room. "The gang's all here. Who's the wife?"

Phyllis raised her hand and squeaked, "Me. I'm Phyllis Gustafson, Gus' wife. Can you fix him?"

## CHAPTER 39
### Audrey

Dr. Lewis also had a stethoscope encircling her neck and a large clipboard in her hands. Tall with a cocky presence, she took command of our group, barreling through us, like a ringmaster at the circus, aiming herself toward Gus. Her height was disproportional to her weight, and her red pants emphasized her ample hips and thighs. She covered her sizable bust with a taut rhinestone-embellished t-shirt topped by a white coat. She had pulled her black curly hair into a chignon held in place with rhinestone clips.

Logan moved toward her saying, "I'm a retired podiatrist. How can I be of service to you or your staff or Gus?"

"Thank you for that, Dr. Hall," Dr. Lewis exclaimed. "The best thing you can do is get these folks out of this room. They are in my way and aren't doing the patient any good either. Everybody should leave, go away, even you, Ms. Phyllis. And especially you, Dr. Hall."

Logan looked around the group, "Sure, we'll all go upstairs and grab some coffee or an adult beverage. Let's get out of the doc's way." He started ushering them out but turned back to Dr. Lewis and said, "By the way, Doc, I checked his feet and for the record, they're fine. No irregularities whatsoever. Well, maybe the start of a corn on his left big toe, but I'll talk to him about it when he gets over his heart attack issues."

Griff glanced back at me and smiled before placing his arm around Phyllis, gently leading her toward the elevator. Carlee moved forward and embraced Phyllis' other side with Steve taking up the rear. The elevator door chimed open and adding the four filled it to capacity. Logan and I remained outside to await its return. Griff called out the door, "Audrey, Big Dipper Bar, top deck."

I gave a little wave in response and the elevator door closed. Logan and I remained quiet; both of us feeling awkward, but a few moments later, the elevator door slid open, and Logan punched six on the keypad. "Let's stop at my room for a minute. I need something," Logan said.

"I hope you don't have an ulterior motive," I answered, wondering if he was going to try to seduce me again. "Maybe I should join the others at the Big Dipper while you get whatever it is you forgot."

Logan explained, "I noticed an irregularity of your feet when I examined them earlier, and I want to recheck, if that's okay with you." His hand shook as he swiped his key card to the panel, and it flashed red three times, before the green light flashed on.

"What about my feet? I know I don't have a bunion like Griff does, and I am pretty sure I don't have athlete's foot or a hammer toe. So, what is this irregularity that you are talking about?" I asked, unsure if I should be alarmed or if he was talking about something else. It was something else.

"No, what's wrong with your feet is that they drive me crazy," Logan pouted as he entered his cabin. "Absolutely crazy."

I knew if I went into his cabin, I would succumb to his increasingly appealing attempts to seduce me, so I said, "I'll wait outside, thirty seconds, and I'm leaving."

## CHAPTER 40
### *Griff*

The Big Dipper was a piano bar that played country music from the fifties, sixties, and seventies. The pianist took requests, and when the first notes of John Denver's *Rocky Mountain High* were played, Phyllis stood, grasped Griff's hand, and sadly laughed, "C'mon Griff, this is our song, Gus and me, that is, and I want to dance. I can't do anything about Gus, but I need to get rid of some of this anxiety. Not *cuchi-cuchi*, like Charo, just dancing." Phyllis and Griff moved to the dance floor. She had hoped for a repeat with Griff, but tonight wasn't the time, but dancing is just dancing, she reasoned.

Griff complied, and once they reached the dance floor, they both tried to figure out if it was a slow-dance song or a fast one. They played it by ear and did both. Breathless, they collapsed into their chairs.

Carlee said, "My turn, Griff. I claim the next dance on your dance card. Steve's not a dancer, but I am. He says he can't hear the music well enough right now but even when he has hearing aids, dancing is not his thing."

Griff looked at Carlee and thought *she's not half bad, a little wrinkly, more wrinkled than either Audrey or Phyllis, but she has a killer figure.* "That would be fun, let's dance," he urged as the pianist began to play *Crazy* by Patsy Cline. Griff led Carlee out to the dance floor and took her in his arms.

Phyllis ordered a gin and tonic with extra lime and said to Steve, "That was a good distraction, but I am worried about Gus. I'm going to find some Xanax for myself."

Steve nodded, "Okay, do you want me to go with you?"

"No, I'm fine, I'll be back in a jiffy."

The music rolled on and Griff and Carlee finished their fifth dance and looked around for Phyllis, "Where did Phyllis go?" Griff asked Steve.

"Oh, she went to get a tampax, she'll be back soon."

"What?" Carlee asked, "A tampax? She's a little old, isn't she?"

The music started again, and Griff and Carlee took to the floor, this time *Gentle on my Mind*, a nice and slow Glen Campbell hit, and they appreciated the gentle rhythm. Carlee, nearly Griff's height, was a graceful dancer. She had laid off the wine since dinner, and he fully appreciated her funny, naughty, and bold chatter. Griff laughed at her repartee. She was as uninhibited a person as he had ever met.

"I wonder what happened to Logan and Audrey? They haven't come upstairs," Griff asked as the song finished. "Maybe I should go on a search."

Carlee had swooned over Griff since they met at the Navy reunion and didn't want him to switch his focus from her, "They are probably just fine," she told him, and then rambled on as a distraction. "This bar is the best of all of them. The maroon velvet chairs remind me of a brothel, although I've never been in a brothel. Aren't you crazy about the music of the fifties and sixties? I know one thing, it's better than being in your fifties and sixties. I'm fifty-nine, sweating in places I didn't know I had, and now I want to take my clothes off all the time. Hot flashes, chills, repeat, repeat, repeat. Age is only a number, but it comes with so many misgivings. My mother told me to *welcome the wrinkles, bring 'em on, they are better than being six feet under.*"

Griff laughed heartily at her spicy comments and added, "I look at getting old this way, when you become a geezer, you get discounts on movies, restaurants, and even the grocery stores have ten percent Tuesdays. You can fart or fall asleep or forget things and nobody cares. Like you said, you can take your clothes off whenever you want, so how about taking your clothes off now?" Griff didn't actually think she would, but it never hurts to try. He had plenty of blue pills left.

"I might be persuaded, but probably not here in the bar. I used to laugh about that Richard Simmons show, *Sweating with the Oldies*. Little did I know I would be the one sweating with an oldie every time I have sex with old Steve. He's seventy-eight and occasionally has an al dente noodle, but most times it's overcooked, you know, it doesn't quite clean the cobwebs from my foo-foo. And I have needs."

Feeling even more confident, "I have needs, too, and wouldn't mind cleaning your cobwebs with my broomstick," Griff offered with a laugh. "I can show you our suite where you can take off your clothes and we can talk about Italian food while you check out my noodle, the one that is becoming more al dente by the minute, by the way. How does that sound?" *It doesn't hurt to try,* he repeated in his brain.

"Really? What about Audrey and Logan?" Carlee asked, peering at all the exits. "We haven't seen them since we brought Phyllis upstairs."

"Audrey's probably getting ice cream. She's on this ice cream kick, it's an obsession. She never eats ice cream at home, but here she has to have it morning, noon, and night." *Three-a-day,* he silently lamented. "Our suite's two floors down, and if you are game, you and I can have a quickie and get back here lickety-split," Griff encouraged.

"But what about Steve and Phyllis? I don't want to leave Steve to deal with Phyllis' grief and this can't be any fun for her," Carlee commented.

"Steve thought Phyllis would be back soon," Griff urged, "We'll make it a quick quickie."

Carlee thought about it briefly saying, "I'll tell Steve I'm going to the bathroom, and he won't know the difference, so you're on. We had an Italian meal earlier, and I'm ready for seconds. I guess it's similar to Chinese food and doesn't stay with you. More noodles, and make them al dente, please," she flirted.

# CHAPTER 41
## *Griff*

Carlee seemed to have no inhibitions, but nothing too brazen or taboo. She facilitated their lovemaking and showed him places and things of which he had no knowledge. Married to Audrey for nearly fifty years, Griff assumed all women felt the same as she, interested in, but not obsessed by, sex. But then, he and Phyllis had wiggled and wriggled, and now Carlee. Audrey never refused him but had never taken the lead either. Maybe Audrey was a cactus in a flower garden, a prickly pear when it came to sex. He had thought she had learned it in her long-ago high school sex-ed class listed under the category *How to Be a Wife*. And it stuck.

Carlee, however, was the opposite, aggressive, active, and adventuresome, like Star Trek, where no man had gone before. He had considered himself passionate, but she knew more about sex and libido than he had ever dreamed of. She crossed lines he didn't know existed and surprised him and his libido again and again in their fifteen-minute workout. He thought, *No wonder poor old Steve is impotent, she wore him out. When you're sitting in the saddle, a horse can only take so many laps around the barn.*

"Do you want lotion?" he offered, remembering Audrey had packed lubricant in their suitcase.

"What for? Not me, I got this," she flirted.

She touched and kissed and whispered in every orifice of his body, not caring what he thought or wanted, only what pleased her. It was a drastic turnaround from Audrey and for that matter, Phyllis, who had surprised him by giving him enormous pleasure one day before.

The three women were as different as owls, cats, and hyenas. Audrey was caring and gentle; Phyllis was surprisingly sexy; but Carlee was wild and wonderful and carried him to the peak of excitement, not once, not twice, but three long, hard explosions, moving his already al dente noodle to uncooked, stiff, and stand-up-straight spaghetti, ready to be plunged into her boiling beaver dam, hotter than any he had ever felt.

She whispered, "Let me, let me. You don't have to do anything, Griff, let me please you." It was obvious she gained pleasure from her movements, transferring her excitement to him, equating greater pleasure for both.

Panting, he gurgled, "Okay, okay, you do it," and he relaxed and accepted her advances for the third time.

When they finished, they both lay on the bed, exhausted. "What did you think?" she cooed. "We matched: same arousal, same climax, we climbed Pike's Peak together. Three times."

"Lionel Richie crooned, *You're once, twice, three times a lady*. Three times, that's a record for me, and I thought this would be a quickie," Griff panted, reaching over and touching her face, stroking it gently.

"Do you like my face?" Carlee asked as he petted her face and neck. "My skin became lined with wrinkles early, and I have tried many products to rid myself of them, but I have finally discovered the secret. I read about it online, saying it is the solution to dry, wrinkly skin. I tried it and could hardly believe the results because it's cheap and over the counter, available at any drug store. I should have had a before-and-after picture taken with the changes I saw."

Griff looked at her, still seeing creases on her face, "It seems soft enough. Wrinkles come with experience and wisdom so don't worry about them. Some people have lots and others don't have any. What type of cream is it? I have a couple forehead lines that I wouldn't mind disappearing."

Carlee answered, "You'll never believe it, it's hemorrhoid cream. Over the counter, plain, old-fashioned hemorrhoid cream."

Griff withdrew his hand, turned over, and closed his eyes. *Eeowee.*

## CHAPTER 42
### *Gus*

Gus finally rallied after dozing for several hours. When he awoke, he was alone and disoriented with kinks and clutter swirling around his brain, until he finally recalled he was on a cruise, had fallen down, and been brought to the clinic. *Where was Phyllis?*

He looked around the room, noting a bunch of green machines and an IV in his arm. He was covered with a sheet, and seemed to be naked, except for his toes sticking out from the bottom of the sheet. He didn't see his clothes, and he didn't see Phyllis. He tried to sit up on the bed, actually a gurney, but his considerable girth gave him little room for maneuvering, so he didn't make much progress. Plus, someone had strapped him to the table impeding his movement.

Dr. Lewis heard him rattling the straps, trying to release himself, and entered the room. "Whoa, there, big fellow, you're not going anyplace. You're staying right here, rocking and rolling with me for at least for one night."

"Who are you?" Gus asked, while trying to sit up. *She looks like a doctor but that can't be. A female doctor won't do at all. Time to get out of here.*

"I'm Dr. Lewis, the ship's doctor, and you have a little problem: a little heart issue, maybe a little heart attack, maybe a little something else, followed by a little fall, and you just woke up from a little nap. So, rest easy, my friend, and let me take your little vitals," she coaxed as she helped him lie back down.

"You can't be a doctor because you're a woman, so don't boss me

120

around. I want to get up and see my wife. Where is she? Why isn't Phyllis here?" Gus avoided doctors, especially women doctors, and this one did not suit him at all.

"Guilty as charged. I'm a woman and a doctor, and I'm here to boss you around. And I'm gonna continue. Hang on, and I'll call your wife. I didn't have to give you the defibrillator, which I call the hearty-starty, so that's a good thing. Your friends accompanied your wife upstairs to get a pink drink to calm her down. She wanted to stay, but I wouldn't let her. And I'll tell you another thing, you have the dinkiest ass I've ever seen," she asserted. "I adore big asses, but yours is kinda cute as old dinky asses go."

She read his vitals and frowned, "Your vitals are jumping all over the place, like snakes with the hiccups. You aren't going anywhere for a while."

"I am fine," Gus grunted, again attempting to swing his legs off the bed. "I need to get up and move a little bit. Would you unfasten this belt? It's binding my gut."

She gazed at him, head to toe, deciding what to say, "No, what you need to do is lose about half of your body weight and if you do, I guarantee you won't miss it. Losing weight is not the same as losing your keys or your hat or even your wife. If you lose your keys or a hat, you go nuts, searching for them all day long, but if you lose your spare tire, in your case, two spares, you'll never look back. And then, Mr. Gus, your belly will match your cute little ass."

He groaned a laugh at her way of putting things, but countered, "We've talked about it, but no, Phyllis and I are not dieting. Neither of us has any interest in starving ourselves."

"Mr. Gus, you need to quit thinking about weight loss as dieting and begin to believe it's a new lifestyle. Get on the bandwagon or you can hand in your lunch bucket. Permanently. Capeesh?"

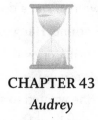

# CHAPTER 43
*Audrey*

I must be an easy mark because Logan invited me to take one more stroll around the ship, and I went with him, even though his incessant attempts to seduce me were a little embarrassing. I honestly enjoyed them, but still, I was determined they weren't going anywhere. The gentle breeze and the night air were pleasant, and I must have been hungry for non-barnyard air because I didn't hesitate and took deep breaths of the sea air. We passed several people, couples, and groups, who were doing the same thing as we were, enjoying the ship's sway and the cool air. We completed two laps before ascending the stairs to go to the Platinum. *Free wine was calling*, Logan laughed, and we asked for plastic glasses, so we could continue our stroll.

"I want to find out more about Lisbon," I told Logan. "We came in such a hurry I didn't have time to investigate, so do you mind if we duck into the library to see what they have?"

"Of course not," he said. The library was open but empty, and I quickly located a book called *Lisbon Live* and checked it out. It was filled with suggestions of things to do. We would only have one day in Lisbon, so we would have to make it count.

I split off from Logan because I wanted to take my new guidebook to our suite, so I could read it at my leisure tomorrow. Reading was a good way to pass time, away from both my husband and my new shadow. I enjoyed Logan and hadn't rebuked him, and true to his word, he wasn't giving up, that was for dang sure.

I scolded myself, *I have to pay more attention to Griff and less attention to Logan, or Griff will get suspicious and all hell will break loose. If only Griff would treat me like Logan treats me. But maybe I don't want that. If Griff thought I had a toe fetish, he would be sucking on my toes all day, and I might have a twenty-four/seven toe-gasm and launch myself into a permanent meltdown.*

I was entering the elevator when I arrived on the tenth floor, running smack dab into Carlee. "Audrey! I'm glad to see you. We wondered where you went. While you were gone, I borrowed Griff to dance, but after a few dances, he wanted to look for you in your suite. When he didn't come back, I came down to check on him, but he didn't answer." Carlee was lying as though her pants had caught on fire, trying to cover her passionate tryst with Griff. "Let's go shopping," she suggested. "Griff didn't answer the door to your suite a second ago and is probably asleep. He looked worn out. So, this is our chance to explore and the jewelry shop is open with nice, expensive jewelry on sale to check out. The key word here is expensive."

"I wouldn't mind, but first let me put this book away. I'll sneak in and won't disturb him," I answered.

Carlee panicked slightly as she had left Griff on the bed, naked and spent, and she doubted he had dragged himself to his feet yet, and offered instead, "No, bring it with you because I want to learn a little about Lisbon, too. We can have a coffee and look it over."

The elevator stopped at every floor, taking its leisurely time to descend to the main deck and we exited the elevator at the same time Phyllis was getting on. I asked, "How is Gus? Any better?"

"I haven't seen him yet. I forgot which floor the medical clinic is on, so I retraced my steps from the dining room and here I am. Now I remember it's on the second deck, and I'm on my way to see him," Phyllis explained. "I miss that old coot."

Carlee and I browsed the shops, checking prices and quality of the gems, but neither of us bought anything. We ordered lattes and thumbed through *Lisbon Live* trying to identify what we wanted to see or do in

Lisbon. None of us spoke Portuguese, and we hoped the Portuguese spoke English. At one time, I had been fluent in French, but other than watching an occasional subtitled French film, I had not used it since college. I sometimes practiced on the chickens, pretending they were French hens, my *faverolles*, but they neither listened nor bothered to correct my grammatical errors.

"We missed the show tonight," Carlee said. "Steve probably wouldn't have gone anyway. Without his hearing aids, he doesn't have much interest in anything, including me. He's become an old fogey since his last birthday, often telling me that he's ancient, not wanting to do anything, including checking out the hidden valley, and I don't mean salad dressing. We haven't done it in a long time. I'm not sure he even can do it anymore."

"Doesn't he take the blue pill?" I asked. "It's helped Griff, in fact, maybe it helps him too much. You've heard him talk, chugga-chugga, three times a day whether I want it or not."

"Griff takes an ED pill?" *Oops,* Carlee thought, *don't say anymore.* "Steve doesn't take anything, and his sex drive has fallen into a pit, a deep and wide pit, but sadly, not my pit. He says, and I quote, he *doesn't want to take any more damn pills because he can't get the damn lids off the damn bottles.*"

I nodded, "I can identify with that because I can't get them off either. Yes, Griff plays the magic blue kazoo, as he calls it, and has a couple other over-the-counter ED pills as well, although he denies it. On top of that, he can be a hypochondriac at times, fearing he will catch any disease he reads about. For example, our closest neighbor who lives six miles from us, has macular degeneration, so Griff heard about it and all of a sudden pinned graph-like papers in every room of our house, because Bill told him if he stared at grids, he would reduce the chance of losing his sight through macular degeneration. Now we have paper grids pasted to the walls of our house, the bathrooms, the back door, the refrigerator, by the telephone. We checked with the ophthalmologist, but he shows no sign of the disease, but he's on the alert and has me staring at least once a day, less often than he wants to chugga-chugga."

Carlee asked, "What about Logan? He seems attentive to you. What's his game?"

I knew enough to be cautious because Carlee didn't know Logan was trying to romance me. "I don't know. We've talked about several things, but he mostly wants to talk about feet. He loves feet, seems almost obsessed with them."

"I noticed he watches feet, yours especially. Does he have a foot fetish? That would be a riot, a podiatrist with a foot fetish," Carlee remarked.

"I asked him about foot fetishes one time, and he started talking about toes, but he didn't answer my question." I recalled Logan sucking my toes and how much pleasure I had taken in it. *What if I had a foot fetish? That would certainly explain my sudden interest in having my toes sucked.* I blushed but prayed Carlee would assume it was only another hot flash.

## CHAPTER 44
### *Gus*

D r. Lewis had given Gus food for thought, change your lifestyle or die, and he lay on the bed mulling over her comments. Gus abhorred doctors and stubbornly resented them telling him how to live his life, yet, this doctor had laid it on the line and oddly enough he didn't begrudge her words. She was a woman and a doctor, and the two should not be used in the same phrase, especially when it came to his health, but she had laid it out in a way that made sense.

Phyllis rapped on the door to Gus' room and poked her head around the corner. "Gus, Darling, how are you? I've been worried about you, but they didn't want me to wake you. I've been up in the Big Dipper Bar with the gang, but it's not the same without you. Have you seen the doctor?" He lay naked, covered by a sheet with a safety belt around his middle. Phyllis lifted a corner of the sheet and smiled, "Looking good."

Gus took her hand, "Yes, Dr. Lewis has dropped by a couple times. Did you know she is a woman? She told me I need to lose weight and take better care of myself, maybe get more exercise. You know how I hate to diet, but I don't want to end up attached to tubes and machines and crap like that. It would be bad enough to wear an emergency button around my neck. That's not a good way to live."

"No, neither of us would want that. I was scared you were going to die," Phyllis whimpered, clutching his hand. "I don't know what I would do if you…"

"Nobody's dying," Dr. Lewis interrupted as she burst through the door.

"The results of the tests came through from the cardiologist in Miami who assured me that it wasn't a heart attack, merely a panic attack, and you are okay, if you don't overdo it. But I'm serious about you losing weight. The next time you might not be so lucky. Tonight, you can spend the night with your wife instead of me, Gus, but I want you to report to me first thing in the morning, not later than nine a.m. No stairs, no gym time, and no shooting the moon with your beautiful bride. Take it easy and you will be able to get off the cruise ship upright, not in a body bag. Also, no alcohol, no dancing, no heavy meals. Eat a light meal, a salad with oil and vinegar dressing or a boiled egg. Deal?"

"That's wonderful, isn't it. Gus?" Phyllis squealed, grinning widely. "We're the luckiest of anybody."

Gus frowned, "It's not so wonderful, Phyllis. Good God, it'll probably kill me: no sex, no booze, no nothing. I'm not fond of salads, and I hate boiled eggs, you know I do. That's a prescription for the dead or dying, not me."

"Guess what: You aren't dead yet, but you could be if you don't adhere to my recommendations," Dr. Lewis said bluntly.

"C'mon, Gus, let's get out of here and tell the others your good news," Phyllis exclaimed. "Let me help you get dressed."

## CHAPTER 45
*Audrey*

"Are you sure you want to do this?" Phyllis asked Carlee and me at breakfast. "We'll have to walk around the ship about twenty times to log five miles in order to earn a t-shirt. That's a lot of walking in this wind." The ship had sped up to outrace a northbound storm, and the wind had really kicked up. It was sure to be chilly.

"I want a Fast Feet for Charity t-shirt to show my kids when we get home. It has the ship's logo and autograph of the ship's captain. It'll be a great memento of the cruise, and it's free," I reminded her.

Carlee chimed in, "Plus the ship gives us a glass of champagne when we finish, and we'll eat lunch with the captain, and they are sure to serve wine with the meal."

Phyllis countered, logically, "It's not exactly free. Let's see, we pay fifty dollars to walk five miles for a three-dollar t-shirt and a glass of cheap champagne. We get our meals anyway, and personally, I don't care if we eat with the captain or not, and I'd have to leave Gus. There's a good chance he might get in trouble doing something he's not supposed to. He's not back from his morning visit with Dr. Lewis yet." She looked around and saw Griff and Steve at the omelet station, but no Gus.

"I told Steve it was free, and he won't know the difference until we get the bill at the end of the cruise," Carlee whispered. "But even then, he probably won't care."

"And we can take a tax deduction for the donation," I state. "It's for a good cause and will be fun. Let's do it."

"Maybe I should wait for Gus," Phyllis said, hesitantly. "I am so worried about my poor baby."

The loudspeaker announced the Fast Feet for Charity event would start in an hour, so we raced to our cabins to trade our vacation wear for tennis shoes and a sweatshirt.

Phyllis picked up her participant's vest but didn't go to the starting lineup. She returned to the cafeteria where she found Gus sitting with Griff and Steve after his visit to Dr. Lewis. Steve and Griff had opted for the kitchen sink omelet with every ingredient imaginable, while Gus had begrudgingly selected a low-fat yogurt and banana. "The doc told me to watch what I eat, but this isn't going to fill me up," Gus groused keeping one eye on the kitchen sink omelet and side order of bacon that Steve and Griff were wolfing down.

Steve reminded Phyllis, "You are going to miss the race. You'd better go."

Phyllis looked at Gus and sighed, "You are right, will you behave yourself, Gus, if I go with the girls? No drinking. No shooting the moon with some other woman. And no dancing girls, you got that?"

Steve said, "I'm finished with my breakfast and want to see the start of the race. I'll walk with you, Phyllis."

"Okay," she answered, pecking Gus on his combover, repeating, "Behave yourself."

## CHAPTER 46
*Phyllis*

Phyllis walked ahead of Steve to the elevator. "I need a hat," she said. "We need to take a little detour. I'm down one floor, but it's near the elevator so won't take long, and I'll hurry."

When they arrived, Phyllis invited Steve in, "Come on in, I'll be only a minute and we can get back to the race. I'm not sure where my hat is, but I'll be quick because there's no time to be wasted."

She used the bathroom, applied sunscreen, dabbed on a fresh coat of lipstick, and located her hat. "I'm ready," she called coming out of the bathroom. "Let's go, as I said before, there's no time to be wasted."

She stopped short and looked at Steve who sat on the bed, naked. "What?" she cried.

Steve said, "You said it was time to get naked, didn't you? That's what I did."

"I said, *no time to be wasted*," she answered loudly. "Oh, my, did you… think…what about Gus? What about Carlee?"

"Gus is with Griff, and Carlee's in the race." He rose, and moved toward Phyllis, cradled her face in his hands and kissed her.

In a slight state of shock, she surprised him by unceremoniously embracing his bare torso and lowering her hands to squeeze his butt before stepping out of her shorts. *Oh my, first Griff, now Steve. I'm going to have had them all, the only one left is Logan. But he's a podiatrist.*

They both felt the earth move, and afterwards Phyllis said, "When I asked you into our cabin, Steve, I didn't intend to go belly to belly with you. I wanted a hat because even without the wind my hair is unmanageable, and now, here I am with you, covered only by my incessant hot flashes. It never entered my mind, but there you were, sitting on my bed, naked as mother earth herself and irresistible. I mean, it just happened. You might be deaf, but the rest of you is alive and well and anxious to please. Your deafness hasn't affected your libido or ability to do the horizontal hula because I had a hard time keeping up with you. Despite my multi-layered body, the horizontal hula is so much fun. And you are the best."

"The horizontal hula? Did I hear you right? You make me laugh," Steve said with a grin on his face. "You've been on my mind ever since Gus introduced us at the Navy reunion. You are one sexy woman, beautiful and erotic, wrapped into one spicy package. And funny as clown shoes on a camel. I could get used to you."

"There's plenty of me to love all right," Phyllis quipped, looking down at her semi-naked rolls quivering like the lime gelatin salad she loved to eat. "Gus says saggy, wrinkly skin gives him more to love, and I guess that means more for you to drill. Get it? The dentist drilled me," Phyllis quipped, letting out a large giggle.

"That's exactly what I'm talking about. Not the drilling part, but your sense of humor and laughter. What I see and what you see are two different things, Phyllis. I see sexy, bright, and beautiful with a fantastic smile and laugh. Your sense of humor keeps everyone smiling, but you only see the mirror image of you. But that is definitely not how I see you. And, for the record, I didn't drill you, I made love to you because I wanted to, not because I'm lecherous or horny. Well, maybe I am, but I can have sex with Carlee anytime because she is eager, even over the top, but you are different, and I'm glad we made love. I want to do it again."

"You are one four-star, smooth-talking, stud-muffin, and I'd let you fill my cavity any time" she said laughing. "You already filled it once, but right now, I should find Gus' doctor," she answered.

Steve was puzzled, "Gus' daughter? You and Gus have a daughter on the cruise? That must be interesting."

"No, we don't have any children. I said *Gus' doctor*, you know, Doctor Lewis."

"Phooey on Doctor Lewis. I want to spend a little more time with you," Steve said, rolling on top of her again. "Come here, you sexy woman, let's hu-la-la."

## CHAPTER 47
### *Audrey*

The race was on, and Logan, Carlee, and I started out together, but before we completed a lap, Carlee lagged far behind. A ship-length later, we lapped her, but ten laps more, I slowed down to a limp.

I whined, "Logan, I'm getting a blister on my heel. I bought these shoes a couple weeks ago but haven't broken them in yet. Do you have any band-aids in your medical bag of tricks?"

"Yes, I do, and we're close to the stairs leading directly to my room where I can give your feet a massage and refresh them to prevent further damage," Logan offered, pointing to a door ahead of them.

"Actually, never mind. I have band-aids in my cabin, as well as another pair of tennis shoes and fresh socks," I resisted, certain that he had ulterior motives. "You finish the race, and I'll go to my cabin and get them. I'll meet you on the deck to finish it."

"Not a chance," Logan disagreed, "Blisters can be serious if they aren't treated well, so I will take care of your foot, making sure it doesn't get infected. I promise I won't accost your toes, although they're yearning to be accosted."

"I'm less worried about you than me. I might lose control," I laughed. "Okay, no accosting and no toe sucking for either of us. God, did I say that out loud?"

We looked behind us, searching for Carlee, but she wasn't in view. So, we headed to the elevator to go to deck ten and my suite.

I sat down on the settee, pulled off my shoes and socks and looked at my budding blister. "Oh, ouch, I'm getting a blister on this foot, too. I should have broken these shoes in before we came, but we decided to come so quickly, I didn't have time." I found my band-aid stash and peeled off the protective papers.

Logan took my band-aids from me and set them down before picking up one foot at a time and peering at the blisters carefully on my feet and toes. "Yes, you have blisters, all right, and you're done walking for the time being, doctor's orders."

"I thought you agreed not to accost my toes, and here you are, ignoring your promise. Could you please apply the band-aids before my feet start to shiver and shrink? We need to finish the Fast Feet event," I advised him. "We'll come in last place, and that's not acceptable."

Suddenly, I heard Griff call through the door. He was pounding with a fist, and I was sure people on the floors above and below would hear him. "Audrey, are you okay? I saw Carlee come around twice but didn't see you at all. I lost my key card again; I must have left it in our room. Open the door."

Logan jumped up and hissed, "I'm not going over the balcony again. Once was enough." He grabbed my shoes off the floor and headed toward the closet leaving his shoes by the couch where he had taken them off earlier.

"Okay, get in the closet behind the suitcases. I'll divert him, and when we leave, you can exit the cabin while we're gone. Five minutes." I had turned into Bill Murray of *Groundhog Day*.

I gave him a gentle shove toward my walk-in closet. "There, go in there, and don't come out until we leave."

He wangled behind a suitcase and knelt down causing him to grimace. He squeaked out a moan, "Ouch, dammit, my knees. Damned arthritis," he hissed aloud.

"Shh, be quiet," I ordered. "I'll be quick and talk Griff into going to get a drink or walking me back to the Fast Feet event. I just have to put on my shoes."

I searched for my shoes and became a hyperkinetic maniac trying to find them. I spied Logan's shoes and tossed them into the closet where one bounced off his head, "Ouch." I realized he must have taken my tennis shoes.

"Shh, and give me my shoes," I hissed again, closing the door to the closet.

Shoes and socks in hand, I opened the cabin door to let Griff in. "Blisters. I have blisters and was just fixing them," I explained. "Is Carlee still walking?"

"Carlee stopped for a few minutes to get a drink, but she started up again. I didn't see Logan either. Where is he? I was afraid you and he decided to hike the Appalachian Trail."

"What are you talking about? Appalachian Trail?" I asked.

"That's what Carlee calls having an affair," he responded. "She told me it came from a politician who hid his girlfriend in the Appalachian woods."

I ignored his comment, wanting to change the subject. "Let's go to the cafeteria and see what kinds of desserts they have. I am hungry for pie."

Griff went into the bathroom to pee, and came out clutching a blue pill and a glass of water, "How about we have dessert here, then go for pie? Dessert our way. Damn, you make my juices boil, how about it, Babe?"

The door to the closet crept open, and I saw Logan stirring about, trying to get comfortable behind the luggage. I slammed the closet shut and thought, *I need to get Griff out of the cabin. He's on the prowl, still thinking about sex and wanting his daily quota, but if I can't get him out of here and he finds Logan in the closet, he would definitely throw him over the rail.* I made a break for the door, opened it quickly and said, "Later, let's go see how Carlee is doing."

## CHAPTER 48
*Logan*

Logan heard the door close and started to stand, but his legs had a different idea. His arthritic knees constantly ached but now were on fire and no longer cooperating. He was afraid he would be unable to stand after having been crouched for what seemed like an hour but was probably only a few minutes. *I've fallen, and I can't get up* echoed through his mind, but he didn't have the buzzer and didn't know who to call anyway.

His knees pained too badly to crawl, and he knew he couldn't stand up without some sort of assistance, but he saw nothing to support himself in his attempt to stand, only hangers and backpacks, nothing sturdy. His only option was to butt-scoot out of the closet to the bed or commode, whichever was closest. He looked down at his new lightweight running shorts that cost more than a bunion surgery, fearing they would be ruined.

The words *go naked* echoed in his head, and he thought *why not?* He slid off his running shorts, leaving nothing to imagination. He maneuvered around and began to butt-scoot backwards across the gravelly carpet, underestimating its coarseness. He chirped and grunted a few times as the carpet scraped and scratched his hind quarters and thighs. A few dribbles of blood adhered to the floor, but he didn't realize he was bleeding. The bathroom was closer than the bed, and he continued his journey, hoping he could rise with the support of the commode. His mind was fixated on exiting the suite quickly before Griff and Audrey returned, but panic struck when he heard a light knock on the door.

Sweat poured off him as he boosted himself to his feet and twisted to view his backside in the mirror. He inspected the damage and noted spots and streaks of blood.

He heard the door open and Ruth, the attendant, calling out "Housekeeping." Still staring at his bloody backside in the mirror, he realized his new running shorts still lay on the closet floor.

"No, not now," he called out, in his best imitation of Griff, hoping Ruth hadn't already entered. Thankfully, he heard the door shut, and he dashed to the closet. He slipped back into his shorts, speckling them with dots of blood. He was overjoyed to be able to stand and walk, even though his unsteadiness made him wish he had Gus' cane as both knees screamed with pain.

Uneasy at his being caught in Griff and Audrey's cabin, he decided he would have to chance it. He turned the knob, squinted through the narrow opening and seeing no one, squeezed himself into the hall.

He eased down the hall to the Platinum Lounge, initialed Griff's name, and asked for a drink. "Scotch, rocks, a double," he stated, "I could use a Scotch."

The hostess answered, "Yes, sir, Mr. Lyon, right away."

He sat down gently, hoping blood wouldn't seep through his clothes to the upholstered chair, and gulped his Scotch, relaxing as the liquid entered his body. He wanted to expel Audrey and Griff from his mind. *Maybe just Griff.* Audrey was lovely, maybe more than lovely, and he thought her interesting, but he wasn't one to break up a half-century marriage, and his rejection rate was bordering on a hundred percent. So far, his attempts had been a disaster, like the sinking of the Lusitania.

Joan had been gone four years, four long years without passion, sex, or companionship. Even conversation, except for the few gold diggers who eagerly pursued him, hoping to take advantage of his financial success and social acumen. Or the many who had foot issues and saw a way to a cheap foot fix.

"Logan, are you okay?" Logan looked up from his drink as Griff and

I approached him. I started, "We saw you sitting alone and thought you might need company. It's difficult to travel alone. We know you have access to the Platinum, so Griff and I signed in as your guests, I hope you don't mind. Griff, could you order a glass of wine for me and another drink for Logan, whatever he is drinking. Tell them to put it on our room number."

With Griff out of earshot, I blurted out, "I tried to divert Griff, but couldn't find an easy way to do it. He's all about his three-a-days." I regretted saying it as soon as the words fell out of my mouth, but I couldn't call them back.

Logan perked up from his negative thoughts and whispered, "Patience, Grasshopper, I have a plan, and it will help alleviate the pain from his bunion."

Griff sat down between the two of them. "You have a little blood on your leg. Did you bump into something?"

"It's only a bug bite, I'm okay," Logan insisted, dabbing at one of the many blood spots on his legs and shorts.

"You must be a high roller to have gotten access to the Platinum Lounge, it's first rate. Say, Doc, when will you look at my bunion?"

## CHAPTER 49
### *Audrey*

"What are you wearing to tonight's dinner? It's formal night," Carlee asked at breakfast the day after the Fast Feet for Charity event. "I brought two evening gowns because I couldn't decide which to wear. One is strapless, and it unfortunately displays my turkey neck, but Steve likes it. The other covers my wrinkled wattle, but it's short and backless. The only problem with that is that it's a little chilly, and I didn't pack a shawl."

I flipped my head to look at Carlee, "Evening gown? What are you talking about? I didn't pack an evening gown. Do we need one for dinner tonight? What do I do?"

"Yes, it's a formal night and nearly everyone will be dressed to the nines. If you want to eat in the dining room, they require you to dress up, but you can eat in the Broadway wearing whatever you want," Phyllis told me. "If you didn't bring formal attire, what about Griff? Does he have a tux? Most people attend the galas, and it's fun to see everyone dressed up."

I burst out laughing at the thought of Griff in a tux, "Griff in a tuxedo? You must be kidding, he's a soybean farmer. We decided to come on the cruise on the spur of the moment, and I didn't even think about packing formal attire. In fact, he had gobs of manure on his shoes when we arrived in Fort Lauderdale. First cruise, remember? The formal night will be wonderful, but what can I do?"

"I only brought one gown, and Gus brought a suit, not a tux, but

139

they'll let him eat in the dining room if he will wear his suit coat. He had an elegant tux, but it either shrank or he grew. Guess which one," Phyllis griped.

"The shops carry a few gowns, at least they usually do, but they don't have much variety. You can rent a tuxedo for Griff if they have his size," Carlee explained. "We should go shopping!"

Three shops carried clothing items, but two sold only sports clothing, shorts, t-shirts, bathing suits, and jogging gear. The third shop held promise for a suitable gown for me, even though the variety of gowns was disappointing. I tried on two gowns and both fit. A long, black dress, strapless, nearly backless molded to my body perfectly and I loved it, but I feared I wouldn't get to wear it, because oversexed Griff would salivate over my bare skin, and he wouldn't be likely to escort me to the dining room without frolicking in the hay. The other choice, a scarlet, sequined, mini dress with sleeves, a back, and a neckline, clung to my body like icing on a cake and I loved it, too. I idly wondered what Logan would prefer and thought the red, because he could see my feet and legs. *Black: Griff. Red: Logan.*

We turned our eyes to the tuxedo rack. I had been buying Griff's clothes since we were married and had no trouble with the size, but unfortunately all the tuxedos had been sold or rented. I spied a lightweight dinner jacket with matching cummerbund and black slacks, a perfect match for my dress. I knew he would like it and decided to purchase it rather than rent it, giving ammunition for another cruise. "I'll buy these," I told the clerk, handing him my key card for payment. "I hope my husband likes them," thinking of both men.

# CHAPTER 50
*Audrey*

Logan phoned and invited Griff and me to join him in the Platinum Lounge for a drink before dinner and Griff observed, "Logan must be loaded. He has the private lounge and buys us drinks and bottles of wine. I should have been a foot doctor because they must make a bundle."

"You hated biology, remember?" I reminded him.

"That's true, but I love money," he countered. "He hasn't examined my bunion yet. Maybe tonight."

"No, Griff, you aren't asking him to look at your bunion while you are dressed up. No way," I scolded. I couldn't believe his bunion had crossed paths with his brain.

Griff looked at himself in the mirror, admiring what he saw, "I don't look half bad in this dinner jacket. I dressed up like this in 1963 when I went to the junior prom with...I forget her name...she's in your bridge group. I told you the story about how she invited me to her prom, right?" Even though I had heard the story a dozen or so times, he continued. "I didn't go to Hunter High School, but I only lived thirty miles west. My mom rented a black tux with a black cummerbund and tie for me because it made her think of Sean Connery in the movie *From Russia With Love*. We're lucky you found one in my size. I know you rented the tux, but did you have to buy the cummerbund, tie, and shoes or could you rent them, too? And when did you get that dress? I've never seen it before, but you look extra hot tonight. Those strapped shoes look nice, too. If we weren't going to the Platinum, we could frolic a bit, which would be much

141

healthier than a drink. I'm ready, let's go."

Griff did look good, handsome and charming, although he added a few pounds under his belt after he quit farming. He resembled Tom Selleck with silver hair, and I had to admit he still had a good poke, albeit with the help of modern medicine. It was the quantity of his pokes I objected to. Between his horniness and my aridness, I felt like I was being pursued by a scorpion on a sand dune. "Her name is MaryBeth Eaton, and she's married to John Eaton, the butcher. I'm glad you like the dress, but is it too tight?"

"No way, it is perfect. It shows off your perfect babaloos and appealing tush." He lifted his foot to a stool to adjust his socks.

I did a double take. Horrified, I asked, "Griff, why are you wearing white socks?" He pulled up his pants legs and showed off his knee-length white athletic socks. "You have to change. You cannot wear white socks. You can wear either black or red, which do you want?"

Griff insisted, "All right, but I don't see what is wrong with them. They are new, right out of the package and nobody is even going to see them. It's not like they have manure on them. I don't see what the fuss is about, but I'll change them if it will make you happy…"

## CHAPTER 51
*Audrey*

Logan rose when we arrived at the Platinum, already having ordered a bottle of wine for me and Griff. He wore a black tuxedo with a red cummerbund and tie and handed me a red rosebud corsage. "Audrey, you look terrific. And Griff, *you clean up really well*, as my mother would say." Returning his focus to Audrey, "Red is my favorite color and, if I might say so, you are red hot, don't you agree, Griff?"

"Yes, I agree, but hot is too mild for how she looks tonight," Griff answered, putting his arm around me and pulling me close.

"Thank you, Griff. Thank you, Logan. The other dress choice was black with large patches of bare skin showing and cost more. I'm glad I didn't waste money on it when you two gave me hot and sexy raves with this little old dress," I answered, smiling, happy they liked it.

Logan added, "It sounds lovely. Maybe you should also buy the black one." Changing the subject, "How have you liked the cruise, so far?"

"It's been full of surprises, that's for sure," I answered, "not that I mind them. I had trouble getting my sea legs at first because of the storms, but I am steady as a sailor now. Walking in the Fast Feet Charity event helped balance me, even though the shoes I wore gave me blisters on both heels, hence backless sandals." Pretending I was Cinderella, I extended my feet out in front of the two men, who both appeared to be drooling.

"Blisters? If they don't heal quickly, let me know, and I'll rub cream on them. I have a cream in my bag that should work well, at least it works for me," Logan offered.

I raised my eyebrows at him in warning, "Thank you, but I'll buy a box of band-aids at one of the shops."

Griff answered, "I've been surprised, too, because things are constantly changing, yet everything is first quality. The food is great, terrific shows, beautiful, but expensive bars, and the music is fun, but I will cringe when I see my credit card statement. And I had to rent a tux and buy shoes, and Audrey bought a dress and shoes, too. We're on our way to the poor house, for sure. And these new shoes are already irritating my bunion. Which reminds me, Doc…"

I interrupted him, "No bunion talk, Griff, and it's only money. Remember your words, *whatever it takes.*" I changed the subject, "I'm happy Gus is better, and thank heavens it was only an anxiety attack, not a heart attack. Phyllis was nearly beside herself. And Steve seems to be having more fun too, even though he struggles to hear. Somehow, something, or someone must have energized him."

Griff inserted, "I think Carlee's having a good time, too."

## CHAPTER 52
### *Audrey*

Both men offered me their arms as we strolled to the lobby, stopping to have a photographer take our pictures. The photographer shot singles, couples, and a triple, plus a couple of silly posed pictures of both men kissing me, one on each side. Without warning, Griff picked up my torso and Logan caught my lower half, and they held me prone in front of them. I squealed when Griff sneaked his hand to my breast at the same time that Logan cradled my toes in his hand in a surreptitious foot massage. Thinking it was funny, the photographer took his time in capturing the moment. Both ends of my body shivered as if I had imbibed an aphrodisiac. Our kids would never believe it, maybe I wouldn't show them that photo. I might be old, but I'm not dead.

When we arrived at dinner, I was still feeling giddy. Phyllis and Gus were already seated, nursing clear drinks with limes in them. Steve pulled out a chair for Carlee and positioned himself next to Phyllis, greeting her by laying his hand on her thigh. She didn't seem to object. Indio and Adie were busy with another table, but Giuseppe appeared with the wine menu. "Who's ordering tonight? I can recommend a wonderful wine if you'd like."

Griff surprised everyone saying, "Tonight's spirits are on me, but Logan can choose. He seems to have a knack for it. But, Logan, I'm a poor soybean farmer, so go easy with my wallet."

"How about we let your lovely wife order? A fine-looking woman can order a fine-tasting wine," Logan suggested. Phyllis and Carlee raised their eyebrows in unison, and Carlee winked at me. Giuseppe nodded and handed me the wine menu. I found a white and two reds that tipped the scale higher than Griff would have liked, but he kept quiet.

After a dinner filled with good food and chatter, we finished the wine and everybody, except Phyllis and Gus, ordered the featured dessert, lemon méringue pie with a dollop of whipped cream.

"It's warm out tonight, so why don't we all go for a stroll outside around the ship? It's good for the digestion, and I haven't gotten my steps in yet," Logan asked, looking at me. "What about it, Audrey, Griff?"

Griff immediately rejected the idea. "Not me. Bunion, remember, Doc? I'm going to go change my shoes and go to the Ocean Waves Bar to listen to a little jazz. You guys get your exercise and join me in the bar for a night cap when you finish your 10,000 steps. I'll get a table large enough for all of us."

"I'm too tired to go on a walk, but you should go," Carlee advised Steve. "I'll go to the bar with you, Griff. We can meet there after you change your shoes."

Gus said, "Not me, doctor's orders, and I need to rest. This is the pits, no dessert, no exercise, no booze, and no hula, but the doc warned me, and it's better than being hooked up to machines or going out on a gurney."

Phyllis agreed, "That's a good idea, Gus, we don't want another episode, but I'm going on a walk. It's part of my new lifestyle. I'm glad I didn't wear high heels."

Steve asked if he could join in, so the four of us, Phyllis, Logan, Steve, and I, set out to cruise around the ship.

We hadn't made a complete lap before I felt cold and was shivering, "I need a sweater. When you mentioned it was warm, you must not have considered the breeze. And, of course, I need ice cream." Logan and I peeled off from the group and began our own path toward a sweater and ice cream and sat to enjoy the sweet treats.

We finished our sorbet in the shop and then made our way to the tenth floor. I opened the cabin door and looked around for Griff before inviting Logan in. Griff's new shoes lay on the floor, and he had tossed his tuxedo jacket, tie, and cummerbund on the bed. He was nowhere to be found.

## CHAPTER 53
### *Phyllis*

"Where did Audrey and Logan go?" Phyllis asked Steve as they reversed directions at the bow of the ship. "They were just ahead of us, and now they aren't. Have you noticed that Logan pays constant attention to Audrey? I wonder if they have something going on?"

"What are you talking about?" Steve asked.

Phyllis spoke louder, "You know, Steve, *cuchi-cuchi*, doin' it, climbing the mountain, just like we did."

"Oh, that Harvey Wallbanger," he laughed. "I doubt it because Audrey and Griff are as straight as an arrow, they're by the book. No fooling around because they would never stray from their vows," Steve explained.

At that, Phyllis found herself reflecting about *Griff being a straight arrow. Since he strayed with me, it's true that he might live by some book, but it's one that is more like* Fifty Shades of Grey.

Steve interrupted her thoughts, "How about this: While Carlee's drinking with Griff in the bar and Gus is asleep, or at least resting, let's go upstairs to my cabin and find something fun to do."

Phyllis was panting by the time they reached the room on the ninth floor. She gasped, "Gus and I tried a silly but fun thing once, but it's risky. When we cruised to St. Kitt's, we had a wonderful balcony. It was warm and breezy, so we emptied the patio of furniture, put blankets and pillows on the floor, and thought we would sleep out there, but one thing led to two, and pretty soon three, and we had sea sex on the balcony. The ocean mist sprayed us at the right time, making it a most memorable moment.

Of course, we were much younger.

"What we didn't know until the next day is that our neighbors had been watching. They were kids, probably in their forties. I overheard them talking, and they called us *chops*, which Gus didn't understand. *CHOP* is text-talk meaning *crazy horny old people*. I suspect they had watched us from the cabin next door, but I was glad they didn't call us *FOPS*. You can imagine what the *f* stands for."

"I'm liking your idea, but it might be too much. I had a hip replacement a few years ago making it tough to get off the floor. But if you lend me a hand, I might be able to manage. I just need to know if it will be worth the effort," Steve replied, moving the two chairs and small table from the balcony to the interior of the cabin while Phyllis stripped off a blanket and pillows from the bed and positioned them outside. Steve peeped around one balcony barrier and whispered, "All clear."

Phyllis laughed, "Oh, yeah, it will definitely be worth the effort. All clear on this side, too."

"Then, Chop-Chop," Steve laughed as he peeled off his pants, and Phyllis echoed his comment as her dress tumbled to the floor.

## CHAPTER 54
### *Griff*

The Ocean Waves Bar was in full swing, and the jazz quartet attracted an eclectic group of cruisers. Some jazz was contemporary, other pieces classical, but it was all sophisticated and well played. The mix of Cuban, Brazilian, and American jazz, along with sassy footwork by the alto sax player, delighted the audience, and they wanted more.

Carlee was pleased to have Griff to herself. Wanting to take full advantage of his attention, she decided to sample his wares. When he drew near, her juices flowed up and down and in and out, igniting her pleasure. She wanted to get to know him better. Being married to Steve had its advantages, free dental care, a fairly sexy meal ticket, and many women who would gladly take her place, but his rapid aging distressed her. Having an *understanding*, in or out of marriage, had crossed her mind because she needed more sheet shaking than old Steve could provide. But she might face obstacles, for instance, Audrey and Steve might want to have a say. The previous encounter with Griff between the sheets had amazed her. She had taken the lead, as was her style, but his full-blooded response had satisfied her more than it ever had with Steve. Audrey had mentioned that Griff used ED enhancement, and it must work because he played well.

"Griff, Audrey seems more interested in her step goal than she is in you. She and Logan have their heads together, comparing notes about their pedometers and healthy eating. Is there something more than cardio and kale going on between them?" Carlee asked innocently. She was sure

Audrey would never have an affair but wanted to plant the seed in Griff's mind. She would have to divert him from Audrey in order to gain his affection and then do the same with Steve.

"No, nothing is going on. She is a married woman. She goes to church every Sunday and would never stray from our marriage. I can count on that," Griff assured Carlee.

Griff was listening hard, so she continued, "Well, you're handsome, smart, funny, and great in bed, such a pleasure in so many ways. You know how to rock the cradle, if you know what I mean, and it's what I want and need. Steve has eighteen years on me and is rapidly approaching eighty. He is aging so much faster than I hoped. His hip replacement slowed him down to a crawl. Life is too short to be trapped in a relationship that isn't working anymore, and I'm considering divorcing him. His three kids aren't fond of me, and they would be glad if I wasn't part of their lives. The same with my five kids. They'd be fine if I got rid of him.

"I'll be sixty this week, and I'm active, wanting more. I want to travel and live the good life. My first husband died and left me with quite an estate of my own. He also was a dentist and invested his money, *decayed teeth money,* he called it, and Salt Lake had massive amounts of decayed teeth. He joked about people *eating more sugar,* but he didn't mean it. So, if I add to that half of Steve's money, if I divorced him, I would have plenty of money to do what I want."

Griff laughed out loud. *Was Carlee making a play for him? He wasn't sure, but it definitely sounded like it. He had never strayed from Audrey until this cruise. Perhaps it was his overuse of the little blue pill or the fresh sea air, but something had snapped. He easily had seduced Phyllis and what seemed like only a few hours later,* Carlee had been willing, too. He looked around for Audrey, but she hadn't returned yet, apparently still out walking with Phyllis, Steve, and Logan. *Carlee was right about Logan though, because he did pay a lot of attention to Audrey. But he was just a boring podiatrist, and Audrey would never...or would she?*

"Eat more sugar? That's a good one. Audrey says sugar is bad for me, but I never thought about my teeth. I thought she meant it would make me fat. You are wrong about Audrey and Logan; Audrey likes to eat healthy food and stay in shape, and she looks good, don't you agree? Especially in that hot red dress." He wasn't really interested in Carlee. She had been a brief diversion, but that was all. Griff looked at Carlee, her wrinkles, and the several empty wine glasses sitting before her, as well as her apparent play for him and thought about something he read years ago, *When asked why he didn't cheat on his wife, Joanne Woodward, Paul Newman commented that it's foolish to go out for hamburger when you have steak at home.* Griff agreed with Paul Newman. *Audrey was better than just any steak though; she was a rib eye.*

## CHAPTER 55
### *Gus*

D r. Lewis insisted Gus return to the clinic every day for her to check his vitals and chide him about his lifestyle. He arrived before the medical center opened every day, first in line. The LPN unlocked the door and invited Gus and other patients in and led Gus to one of two exam rooms. He didn't have to wait long until Dr. Lewis joined him in the room, saying, "Take your clothes off, Gus, I want to check you out." Little by little, Dr. Lewis had won him over, and he enjoyed her bantering about his lifestyle and weight and lack of exercise, but he had never undressed for her. Her request surprised him, but she was the doctor, and Phyllis had cautioned him to obey her.

"Why do you want me naked?" he quizzed as he began to disrobe.

"I want to calibrate you, and confirm you are following my instructions. It's better than a scale, and since our scale only goes to three hundred pounds, Houston, we have a problem."

"Calibrate me? I'm trying, but it's only been three days," he whined, as she lectured him about his spare tires. "I'm starving, and Phyllis is nagging me about dieting, but I hate dieting." He grabbed a towel from a shelf and attempted to wrap it around his lower half, but it didn't go all the way around.

"If you don't want to diet, why don't you try sexercise?" Dr. Lewis asked. "Sex three times a day, morning, noon, and night or more if your heart can stand it." He remained quiet for a minute, wrestling with the towel covering his privates.

"Our friends Griff and Audrey are on that diet. They do it three times a day, and they are both in good shape, at least Audrey is. Griff could lose a few pounds, but he weighs less than I do. He uses a blue pill to help him raise the flag, but Phyllis would never go for that," he said, shaking his head. *But Carlee would,* he thought, remembering her comments about the *old sugar stick.* Not realizing he was speaking out loud, he asked "Does it have to be with the same woman?" *Maybe I could bonk Audrey, too? Probably not though, because she and Griff are as tight as spandex on an elephant.*

Dr. Lewis laughed, "I'm quite sure Phyllis would want it to be with the same woman, *her,* but you know her better than I do. Who do you have in mind?"

"Do we have doctor-patient confidentiality in this conversation, as I stand here pretending to be a centerfold for a lady's magazine? How about Carlee, you know, the one with spiked black hair. She talks about sex all the time."

Dr. Lewis interjected, "That's the best you could come up with? She's cheeky and feisty and not the sharpest tool in the shed. You can do better, maybe you need a smart and sassy chick. Actually, how about me, your ever-lovin' doctor. I'm available. Are you interested?"

"What? You? You like fat guys? You keep telling me to lose my spare tires, so it never occurred to me you'd like the big boys," Gus questioned.

"To the contrary: My mama told me to fall in love with a fat boy who would keep me warm in the winter and give me shade in the summer."

"I've never done it with a doctor, which would take the doctor-patient relationship to a whole new level," Gus said, smiling.

"Just because I tell you to flatten your tire, doesn't mean I don't want to rub the tread." Speaking bluntly, "Yeah, it's an invitation, Gus. I adore meaty men. It's been a while, and the ship's motion has made me a little horny. I want something meaty to grab onto, and I don't mean your love handles."

## CHAPTER 56
*Audrey*

"Griff, wake up," I called from the balcony. "We've arrived in Funchal, Portugal. I want to get off the ship and see all the sites Madeira has to offer. Look at all the boats and how the colorful houses scale the hills. It's spectacular."

"If we get off the ship, what will we do? Drink wine? Shop? People watch? It all sounds dull to me," Griff commented.

"Some of the excursions sound exciting and fun, like the cable car ride with a toboggan sled ride. You told me you weren't interested, so I only bought one ticket. Phyllis is going, and Logan. Gus is staying on board because of his health, and Carlee and Steve didn't say anything."

"Logan's going?" He thought about what Carlee had suggested, and his suspicions heightened. "And Phyllis? He was definitely not interested in Carlee, but he wouldn't mind having another feast of Phyllis and hopping on that train again. "Maybe I should ride the cable car, too. A toboggan ride though? With no snow, how can you ride a sled?" Griff asked me.

"I don't know, but I'm going to do both. We can check out a Gothic church and Madeira's decorative gardens and do some shopping for the grandkids. It doesn't matter what we do, because as long as it is not Hunter, I'll be grateful for whatever we see. Get dressed so we can eat a quick breakfast before we go. I'll stop by the ticket office to see if I can buy another ticket," I ordered. "Hurry up."

\*\*\*

When we entered the cable car, Logan, Phyllis, Mel Black and his dog Jack were already seated. We greeted each other, and Griff wrapped his arm around my shoulders, as if claiming me and leered at Logan, who sat next to Phyllis. I twisted away from him, preferring to view Funchal and the cable car's spectacular view. The steep winding streets and colorful, postage-stamp, flower and vegetable gardens showcased a variety of bright colors as the group floated by cable car high above the city. Precipitous cliffs filled with lush green and yellow shrubbery contrasted with the orange tile-roofed houses. A light rain drizzled down and scented the scenery.

"This is the best thing we have ever done," I told Griff. "Why do we continue to live in Hunter when we could see all these other things. Maybe we can travel full time. We could sell everything and live on a cruise ship or become ex-patriots and live in Portugal or a different warm country."

The cable car stopped at a cavernous, round, 360-degree-windowed building atop a mountain, and we quickly exited. We waited inside until the rain calmed before walking up the street to the steps leading to the Church of Our Lady of Monte. We looked up at the challenge of eighty steep, irregular steps that formed the pathway to its doors. "I'm going to climb the steps to see the church. Anybody else?" I looked around to see if there were any takers.

"Griff and Phyllis shook their heads. Griff said, "Not me, Babe, my bunion hurts, and I'm not going to risk it getting worse."

Phyllis declined also, "Don't they have an elevator? It would be fun to go up, but I'm not climbing those stairs. They don't even have a handrail, and it looks dangerous. No way."

Logan started climbing, "I guess it's Mel and Jack and you and me," he whispered, "Babe," as they scaled the steep and narrow steps, dodging vendors, beggars, and dogs.

The 1500s church was tiny but beautiful with statues of saints clinging to the ceiling, spying on churchgoers from above. Logan and I viewed and admired the intricate architectural design and the complicated glass windows and silver crosses. The view of the bay was delightful, and cameras around us were being clicked. Above the exterior entry way, a small flock of pigeons sat, patiently cooing and staring at us.

By the time we returned from the church, the toboggan team had tucked Griff and Phyllis into one of the traditional wicker sleds, manned by two costumed runners who would push and guide the sled to the base of the hill. The runners had donned blue rain gear to keep dry and covered the riders with a clear plastic sheet for the four-minute slide to the base of the mountain. Gravity and the wet streets allowed the basket to descend the mountain quickly, bouncing and careening from one side of the lane to the other, even turning completely backwards at one point. The stone walls on either side dared the toboggan to veer into them, and Griff and Phyllis gripped each other's hands for the precarious trip down the mountain. Logan and I did the same, laughing the whole trip.

Afterwards, Griff and Phyllis discovered a bistro out of the rain where they waited for us and sipped Madeira wine. "What fun that was!" I exclaimed when we met up with them. "I'd never be able to have this much fun in Hunter. I'd do it again."

"Not me," Phyllis disagreed, sipping her wine. "I almost peed my pants. It was the scariest thing I've ever done. Gus would probably have another heart attack, well, panic attack, which is nearly as bad."

Mel and Jack, last to enter the toboggan, were eager to have a new experience. Jack wore his service dog vest, and Mel held tightly onto the leash as they maneuvered themselves into the sled. The runners warned the pair that the ride might be scary, especially for a blind person, but Mel was confident they could manage the trip and safely descend to the bottom of the route without incident. In all the years they had been together, Jack had never left his side and had never even barked, but he had never been in a toboggan either.

The first few gentle turns allowed the sled to glide down the hill with no problems, although it drifted from side to side, sometimes kissing the concrete walls. The runners guided the sled and gave Mel an ongoing progress report about the trip, even though it was in Portuguese and neither Mel nor Jack spoke anything except English and dog. The runners steadied the sled, keeping it stable. As they started the slide down the hill, Jack emitted a few whines that turned into yawps, and he stood to balance himself. One of the runners tried to make him lie down as they entered a steep hairpin curve, causing the toboggan not only to pick up speed, but to swerve. The wall kissing became wall slicing and Jack flew out of the sled, nearly taking Mel with him. Mel caught himself and released the leash as he did, ejecting Jack from the ride. Jack slammed into the concrete wall nose first and scrambled to retain his footing, but the road was wet and slippery, and he continued to slide down the hill, grappling but finding nothing to stop him.

The runners veered the sled off to the side and radioed the other teams to pause their descent to avoid a collision. They gathered up Jack and placed him on the floor of the sled. He had cut his nose and lip during his adventure and blood dripped to the floor of the sled as he whined in protest. The toboggan completed its ride to the base of the hill without further incident, and Jack returned to his guide dog duties, but not without objection.

"How did Jack do?" I asked Mel, "Is that blood? Is he okay?"

"I liked it, but Jack didn't. He jumped out of the toboggan halfway down and banged his head on the concrete retaining wall. The runners told me he cut his lip, but I can doctor it when we get back to the ship. He's not a happy dog," Mel commiserated.

Griff said, "Now that it's over, I can say that it was fun, but the rain made the street very slick, and we had a couple of real scares."

"I'd do it again because it's the most fun I ever had not dealing with feet," Logan exclaimed.

## CHAPTER 57
### *Audrey*

When we returned from Funchal, we, sans Logan, found ourselves gathered in the Rising Tide Lounge, listening to the Night Sky Trio playing a version of *Sweet Caroline*. The version being sung by the Asian/Latin group sounded quite a bit different than Neil Diamond's version. Half-filled glasses of wine sat on the table in front of us, and we chattered about our day in Funchal.

"Audrey was right, the cable car and toboggan ride down the mountain was fun if you forget about the rain throwing the toboggans out of control. Phyllis and I hung onto each other in case one of us was tossed out," Griff laughed. "But we both would have been launched into a concrete wall on either side of the road, like Jack."

Griff offered, "You should have come with us. We rode a big sled on slick pavement, made slicker by the constant drizzle falling from the sky today. The ride lasted about four or five minutes and was scary as hell, but fun, at the same time. The ride terrified Mel Black's service dog, and he jumped out of the sled and had a bloody nose or lip. I haven't seen him since we returned, so we don't know if he's okay."

"What did you two do today?" Phyllis asked Carlee and Steve.

Carlee answered, "We did a self-guided walking tour of Funchal's downtown and stopped at a couple storefront vineyards to sample their tasty and cheap Madeira wine. We brought back two bottles to share, but the crew stored them and won't let us have them back until we dock in Lisbon. It's a bummer, but at least we can order Madeira at our meal in about an hour."

159

"I need to get cleaned up before we go to dinner," I told everyone. "After the wet toboggan ride, I feel sticky and soggy, so please excuse me. I'll see you all in a bit."

Griff smiled with his eyes pinned to my breasts, "That goes for me, too, hot and wet."

We started for the elevator, carrying our drinks, but as we passed the Platinum, Logan called out, "Audrey, Griff, I hoped you would come by. Won't you join me?"

We stepped into the private lounge and greeted Logan, "Hi, Logan, we were about to get cleaned up for dinner. Why don't you come to our suite while we change into clean, dry clothes? It won't be long. And you can look at my bunion."

Logan declined, "No, I'll wait here. I made a reservation at the sushi restaurant tonight. Do the two of you want to join me? I reserved a table and have already paid the cover charge. I can see if they will make room for two more while you change clothes. I'm sure it won't be a problem."

I smiled, pleased at the thought, "That sounds great, because I've never had real sushi, just what they sell in the grocery stores, so I'm game to try it. If it doesn't taste good, we can go to the Broadway later. Or we can have ice cream. Let's do it, Griff."

"Pass. Audrey, you can go if you want, but I'm not big on raw fish," Griff guffawed. "I want my sushi deep-fried with ketchup, coleslaw, and a side of fries. And a Coors." He grabbed my hand and pulled me toward our suite.

## CHAPTER 58
### *Audrey*

"Well, who are you? Look at this pretty blue bird with the bright yellow belly sitting on our balcony; I wonder what it is," I mused aloud as I pulled the balcony door open. The bird hopped up and down but didn't fly away. Its blue back and wings shuddered as it stared at me through its black bandit-like eye stripe. "This guy is just sitting on our deck watching the world pass by. It doesn't appear to be frightened of us. Have you ever seen one before?"

"Yes, it's beautiful," Griff agreed. "I've seen it a couple of times around the ship, beginning in Fort Lauderdale. I think it's a stowaway."

"A stowaway or maybe a pirate, that's a thought, but with a black stripe across his eyes, he reminds me of a bandit," I laughed. "I'll bet the library has a bird book. I can check there after I eat sushi."

"Are you serious about eating sushi with Logan? I don't care, but do you want to eat fish bait? Do they have ketchup or hot sauce? I learned in the Navy that hot sauce kills the taste of everything." Griff abruptly changed the topic, "Carlee says you are doing the dirty with Logan, but you aren't, are you?"

"No, Griff, of course not. He's a widower and is lonely, and I like him. We have many things in common, like our 10,000 steps, and we both are interested in our health. Besides, he's a doctor, and I can learn by listening to him. I've already learned about feet and toes and other body parts below the waist, I mean below the knees. I'll never see him again after we get off the ship."

"Have you learned anything about bunions? He told me he would help me out, but so far, I've got nuthin'. Could you ask him again about my bunion while you're chowing down on sushi tonight? Maybe you'll have more influence than I do," Griff griped.

"Sure, I'll ask, but don't get your hopes up. You should find him when he isn't doing anything and ask him. I'm sure he won't mind." I encouraged. "By the way, do you think this bird is hungry?"

"Maybe, but what do birds eat? Caterpillars or worms, right? Hopefully there aren't any on board the ship. Fish, maybe. We can try fish if you could bring him bait from the bait bar. We're having lobster in the dining room, but I'm not feeding lobster to this guy. I bet they eat seeds, too. The stewards left peanuts in our bar, and I can crush a couple to see. I'll put a little water in the ashtray on the balcony, too."

The cabin stewards, Alfonzo and Ruth, knocked on the door and requested permission to turn down the beds, and I invited them in. Ruth spied the little blue bird on the balcony saying, "Oh, there you are, you little stowaway. Charlie Parker's back, I thought we had lost him. He's been hiding on this ship since we left Lauderdale. He flies onto a balcony and charms those who coddle him, eats their snacks, poops on the floor, and then leaves. That has been his pattern for the last eight days, and you might be his latest victim."

"What kind of bird is he?" I asked.

"He's a Tenerife Blue Tit bird, native to this area of the world, mostly the Canary Islands. The crew named him Charlie 'Bird' Parker, after the saxophone player from the 1950s," Alfonzo clarified.

"Charlie Parker, the tit bird," Griff repeated, "I've never heard of a tit bird, but it's a great name. I get in trouble with Audrey when I say *tit*, but now I can say it all day long. Tit bird, tit bird. I've heard of the blue-footed booby bird, but a tit bird is even better. These foreigners sure know how to name their birds."

The stewards left, and I moved to the closet to grab a change of clothes. I put on a tiger print skirt I had found at a consignment store and added a black merino sweater I had found on sale at the mall. I hadn't worn either before. I put on black sandals, thought about Logan, and switched to a pair of flats with no toes showing. I didn't want him ogling or sucking my toes in the sushi restaurant.

## CHAPTER 59
*Audrey*

Logan and I strolled toward the sushi restaurant located two decks below at the stern of the ship, and I eagerly anticipated trying sushi that had not been wrapped in grocery store plastic with a $4.99 label attached. Logan, however, wasn't fond of sushi, and had correctly guessed that Griff, a soybean farmer from Idaho, where the trout ran fast and cold, would not be either. Despite what he told Griff and me, he had not reserved a table at the sushi specialty restaurant and had no intention of eating raw fish. He quite agreed with Griff's comment that fish needed to be deep fried with ketchup, especially the ketchup. Instead he linked his arm through mine and steered me toward the bow of the ship, where the spa was located.

He explained, "I confess, Audrey, I hate sushi, but on the other foot, massages give me so much pleasure. The spa has these splendid couple's massages. I am not a couple but wonder if you will join me for one of the best things in life. There is only one thing better, but I'm saving it for later. I already made a reservation for us hoping you would agree."

I was dumbfounded. Hunter didn't have a real spa, only a few homegrown nail and hair salons, and I had never had a massage, let alone a couple's massage. I couldn't imagine Griff wasting money on such a frivolous thing. It sounded sexy beyond words, and as I considered it, my breasts blossomed, and my body's mercury ignited in anticipation. The thought made me a little choked up, and when I tried to talk, I couldn't get anything out, except *roger* with a thumbs-up sign.

164

The elegant spa had a half-circle, white leather couch and a round coffee table centered in the reception area with planters holding ferns on either side. Additional ferns sat on either side of the door. Several wall mirrors expanded the size of the room and mirrored shelves attached to the reception desk held a variety of colorful bottles of lotions. A large cabinet housed towels rolled into loaves.

Micah and Martin, the masseuses, were waiting when we arrived at the spa and showed us thick terrycloth robes available in separate dressing rooms. "What type of massage would you prefer: Thai, Swedish, or Japanese?" Micah asked. "We are trained in all three and are pleased to provide you with your preference."

"What do you recommend for beginners?" I asked, unaware of the differences. As Shakespeare had so eloquently penned, a massage was a massage was a massage.

Martin answered, "Definitely the Swedish massage, because it will relax you and give you energy at the same time. It lasts thirty minutes and you will be covered by an oversized soft towel during the entire procedure, except for the part of the body we are massaging. It's our most popular. And you, Sir, what is your preference? Also, the Swedish?"

"Yes, I definitely want to get rid of my tension and need more energy, so I'll also have the Swedish," Logan agreed.

Micah and Martin assisted us to the tables and removed our robes, substituting bath sheets in a swift, non-intrusive gesture. They pulled the towels back to our waists and asked what aroma we wanted. I thought about what I didn't want and blurted out, "I don't know, but not fish oil, definitely not fish oil."

The two men laughed and sprinkled scents I had never smelled before onto our backs, then began kneading the oils into our skin. My mind returned to Griff, bewildered I had consented to betray him. I was supposed to be eating sushi, and I didn't want to smell like coconut or pineapple or another tropical fruit when I saw Griff next.

After the massages were finished, I shared my thoughts with Logan. "OMG, male masseuses? I never considered the masseuse would be male.

How will I ever explain this to Griff, and what am I going to tell him when he asks about the sushi? Not to mention smelling like coconut," I said. "He is sure to ask."

Logan whispered back, "Tell him you liked it so much that it gave you an orgasm, which we probably can arrange after we're done here."

# CHAPTER 60
## *Griff*

The dinner theme was Lobsters Galore, and every dish started or ended with lobster. Indio, Adie, and Giuseppe, clad in traditional Portuguese costumes, stood ready to serve. The dining room had been decorated with lobster pots and nets with the Portuguese flag gracing every table and wall and the front of the menu read in both English and Portuguese: Celebrate Portuguese Lobster.

"What if somebody doesn't care for lobster?" Phyllis asked.

Gus responded, "Are you kidding? Who isn't crazy about lobster? I could eat two. Or three." He looked at Phyllis and changed his plan, "but I'll make do with one. By the way, Griff, where's Audrey tonight? I haven't seen her in a couple days. I heard I missed out on a dynamite cable car tour and sleigh ride down the mountain. Phyllis couldn't stop talking about it."

Griff commented, "Audrey's eating sushi with the foot guy. It's a nutrition thing. They both have the same idea about raw fish and kale being healthier than lobster with melted butter. She'll probably be starving in the middle of the night, wake me up, and beg me to go with her to the Broadway to eat, and guess what they'll have, leftover lobster. I don't get it."

Carlee raised her eyebrows at Griff saying, "Well, I get it, and I'm surprised you don't. You might say she and Logan have a sticky relationship."

"What did you say? Audrey and Logan are having a quickie? I thought they were eating sushi," Steve commented.

Griff glared at Carlee but decided to hold his tongue. His earlier decision was a good one, but no need to rankle her.

All heads turned, and all eyes focused on Carlee and Steve, and Gus cautioned, "Hold it, Carlee, Logan is a nice fellow, and she's married. We have rules in our society, especially in Idaho. They both know the rules, which are firmly fixed in all our heads. They aren't fooling around, not at all. You can count on it, so let's shift our conversation back to lobsters."

"Rules are changing, just saying," Carlee answered, snidely.

Indio interrupted the conversation, making everyone more comfortable, "So, what may I bring you tonight for dinner? Boiled lobster with butter all around?"

"Yes," they chimed in unison.

Phyllis shook her head, "I'm dieting, so no butter for me, please, but I want to sample the Mexican dishes listed on the menu, lobster quesadillas, lobster tacos, and lobster nachos. Could we share them because I only want a taste? Half-sized would be okay too."

"Of course," Indio agreed. "And lobster salad for everyone? Does anyone want to try the lobster pizza?"

Gus said, "Yes," but noticed a disapproving Phyllis, and followed with, "No, thank you, and no butter for me either."

"Will Miss Audrey and Mr. Logan be dining with us tonight?" Indio asked. "Should I ask the chef to save a lobster for them?"

"Good question," Griff answered, looking first at Indio, then at Carlee. "They are eating sushi tonight, but I know how much Audrey loves lobster. While we wait for dinner, I'll find the sushi restaurant and ask Audrey if she wants one saved for her. I'll be right back."

## CHAPTER 61
### *Griff*

The sushi bar had a queue extending into several waiting areas, scattered through the lobby like a broken humpty-dumpty. A sign announced the current wait time of fifty-eight minutes and a hundred or more people waited, talked, laughed, and drank, but Griff didn't see Audrey and Logan. He ordered a beer from the bar and bulldozed his way to the reception desk, saying, "Excuse me, excuse me," receiving frowns and disparaging comments, ignoring all. The hostess checked her reservation list and didn't find Logan's name, but Griff was welcome to pass through the restaurant in an attempt locate them. *I can't believe this many people prefer sushi over lobster.*

Puzzled that Logan apparently didn't have a reservation, Griff strolled through the main part of the restaurant, eyeing the sushi, and wondering where they kept the ketchup, in case Audrey liked sushi and wanted to come back. He didn't see any ketchup or salsa and retraced his steps through the waiting areas and adjoining bar area, examining faces more closely this time, but no Audrey. He remembered the Platinum Lounge and rode the elevator up and peeked in the door, silently cursing Logan and his extravagance of a private bar. But, again, no Audrey. He checked their suite, but it was empty of Audrey, and the Tenerife Blue Tit had disappeared, but not before depositing a glob of white bird poo on the rail. He climbed two more flights to the top deck to see if they had gone to one of those bars. No Audrey. No Logan. But Charlie Parker, the tit bird, sat next to Mel Black at the bar. Griff sat down next to Mel and ordered a gin and tonic. He looked around the bar, noted the white cane, and asked, "You have another friend sitting here, Charlie Parker, a tit bird. Where's Jack? He never leaves your side; is he all right?"

Mel shook his head, "Jack's asleep in the cabin. When he jumped out of the toboggan, he jarred a canine tooth loose, and it's dripping a little blood. I thought I'd let him rest. I gave him a doggie pain killer, and he conked out. He'll be all right after he rests a little. Until he gets better, I'm on the cane, not the canine tonight." He tapped his white cane on the floor.

"I hope he's better tomorrow, but I'm looking for Audrey, so I need to go now. I will check in on you and Jack later." Griff exited the Night Sky Bar and strolled through the Big Dipper and Sky Water Bars and the common areas. He did not see Audrey or Logan, but noticed Charlie Parker following a few yards behind.

*I give up, maybe Carlee's right, and they are having an affair*, he thought, *No, not Audrey. She could, but she wouldn't. I'd kill her. And him.* He had been gone for an hour and was no farther in his quest. His lobster would be cold, and the others would have already finished eating.

"I give up," he announced to himself and entered the elevator to go the dining floor, weaving his way through the second seating throng. He located their table and sighed that he was correct, everyone had finished, and his lobster was probably cold.

"Did you find Audrey and Logan?" Phyllis asked. "Did they change their minds about sushi and decide to join us?"

"No, I didn't find them, but I found Charlie Parker who has apparently moved out of our room. I checked the sushi place and everything around it, the Platinum, the top deck bars, and our suite. I didn't find either of them. I don't know where else to look."

"Did you check Logan's cabin?" Carlee asked with a cynical sneer on her face, "I'd check there."

Griff looked at her contemptuously, "No, I don't know where his cabin is, and she wouldn't go there, but I forgot to check the ice cream shop. They might be eating ice cream because you know how Audrey loves her sorbet, and it tastes much better than sushi. I should have remembered."

"Miss Audrey, Mr. Logan, we thought we lost you," Adie smiled. "Please sit down."

"I hope we aren't late for dinner," I announced, as I squeezed in next to Griff, "The sushi bar was jammed, and we waited for a while, but decided to forgo sushi in favor of lobster."

# CHAPTER 62
*Audrey*

Having a late breakfast with the girls, Carlee shared brightly, "Today's my birthday, and I'm celebrating two things: my sixtieth birthday and my one-week anniversary of not having a single hot flash. How special is that?"

"You're turning sixty? You are a baby. But, if you lie about your age, you can be any age you want, Phyllis teased. "I only claim to be forty, I figure my aging began when I married Gus, and we celebrated our fortieth last year. I'm just a kid."

I agreed, "That's a thought. My kids think life began when the Internet was born, which would make me only about thirty. You haven't had a hot flash in week? Congratulations. I'm over sixty-five, and I still get them, not every day, but you know, when I least expect it. Yesterday I asked the cruise director a question about how often the Lisbon trolleys ran, but what came out was what *gizmo* to buy because my brain blanked on the words *trolley and schedule*, and the word *gizmo* popped out. I was glad I didn't say *thingamabob*, which might move it to a whole new level. I'm sure he thought I had dementia, but I wanted to know his opinion. I blushed, but without warning: hot flash with red face, sweaty palms, sweat dripping down my forehead, the whole thing. My temperature must have spiked to one-hundred fifty degrees, and it lasted a long time. I left the session before he could answer and beelined it to the ice cream shop, drank three glasses of ice water, and downed two bowls of ice cream."

Phyllis laughed, "I saw you leave but didn't know why. I'm sure he has seen brain blank outs before because everybody our age gets them. My worst hot flash in recent days happened in the Rising Tide on our first day aboard the ship. We were all getting acquainted when suddenly, I bloomed like a cherry tree in April and my upper deck with bees buzzing around. I lost track of my words because I only thought about plunging my head into a freezer or a toilet, whichever happened to be closer. I downed my gin and tonic in a single gulp and crunched the ice and then did the same to Gus' drink. You probably thought I was an alcoholic, but I was on my own private equator excursion. It was awful."

"I started having hot flashes when I was forty, meaning I have been dealing with them for twenty years," Carlee interjected.

"I had early onset of menopause, so lucky me, I began getting hot flashes earlier than most, at thirty-five," Phyllis opined, fanning herself with her hands. "I've been flashing for over thirty hot years."

Carlee continued, "At first, they were almost painful, but later I realized I was becoming more sensual with each of the hot flashes popping up several times a day. Luckily, I wasn't working, because I would heat up and flash like a bonfire, and have a mini orgasm, right there, wherever, whenever, it didn't matter. I called them orgasm-lite because they weren't enough to send me into a full erotic spasm, but, zowzers, they were nice," she laughed. "The minis lasted for a few years, but suddenly stopped one day. I thought I would have to remove my skin to cool down."

"All women ride the hot-flash locomotive, and everybody has her own story. Women are so lucky: periods, birthing babies, menopause, and hot flashes, followed by the Sahara Desert wasteland below the waist. About the same time, we start to dry up, men start with their prostate problems, and we get to help them with those issues," Phyllis said cynically.

My mind flashed to Logan and his continued quest for my attention. Although I tried to expel him from my mind, he kept returning, like the proverbial rubber ball. Even now, talking to the girls, as I thought of him, my female parts quivered, "You are right. Still, what do men go through? They think about sex and little else from when their first zit appears to when their dingdongs fizzle. And when they can't do it anymore, a sympathetic doc prescribes a blue pill and a whole bunch of over-the-counters to help them perform at the same rate they did at age twenty with wives who are forty years older, tired, and disinterested. The drug companies must be earning a fortune from fizzly dingdongs."

Phyllis laughed, "Maybe the federal FDA is text talk for Fizzled Dingdong Administration."

## CHAPTER 63
### *Carlee*

"How are you celebrating your birthday, Carlee?" I asked. "Are you and Steve having a special dinner at one of the fancy restaurants?"

"I don't know. I'd like to go to the steak house followed by dancing, but Steve doesn't seem to want to do anything. He is almost eighty, but he acts like he's a total fossil. Part of the problem is the hearing aid situation, but I'm seeing our eighteen-year-age gap widening every year. It didn't seem like that big of a deal when we first married because he was a flirtatious, a slightly older dentist, and I was forty-two. But the chasm now is deep," Carlee complained.

I said, "I noticed bowling will be available on the Sky View deck, which might be fun. Griff has no interest, so we could do a girls' night out if you are up for that? The boys can have their dogs and brews, and we can go bowling. But be forewarned, with the way I bowl, the ball might roll off the ship and kerplunk a grouper in the head."

"That could be fun," Phyllis agreed, "I like to bowl, but Gus doesn't, and he will want to watch the game on TV anyway."

"A birthday bowling party. Let's do it," Carlee agreed. "Will they serve wine?"

I chimed in, "Of course! They serve wine everywhere. It's practically a cruise ship requirement. And the Sky View deck has several bars."

"What are you girls scheming about?" Logan asked as he passed by. "Are you going to the comedy theater tonight? It sounds fun, but I'd rather be with more people."

"No, we're not going to the theater, though it would probably be fun," I answered. "Today is Carlee's birthday, and we thought we would go bowling on the Sky View deck. Griff hates to bowl and would most likely prefer to watch a ball game."

"Steve is not a big bowling fan either and will plead a hearing disability even though he could bowl without hearing anything," Carlee said.

Phyllis added, "Gus is under doctor's orders, and a college basketball game is showing in the bar, so he won't go either, although he bowled regularly when he was younger. I'm guessing all three of the guys will be in the bar, having a toddy or two."

"You think?" Logan said, "Happy birthday, Carlee. May I join you?"

Suddenly, the loudspeaker squeaked on: *This is the captain speaking. Is there a veterinarian aboard? If you are a veterinarian, would you please contact the front desk?* He repeated the request and waited, re-announcing it after a few minutes.

Logan mused aloud, "I'm not a veterinarian. Do you suppose Charlie Parker is sick? Or maybe Jack? I know Jack hurt his nose, but maybe he hurt his foot, too. I could definitely help if it's his foot, I'm good with those."

A few more minutes passed before the loudspeaker squawked again: *This is the captain speaking. Is there a dentist aboard? If you are a dentist, would you please contact the front desk?*

Carlee nearly jumped out of her chair. "Steve! Where is Steve? He will never hear the announcement, so we have to find him. I'll check our cabin. Phyllis, could you check the casino? And Audrey, could you check the bars on the Sky View deck? He'll be in one of those three places. Tell him he's needed; the captain needs him."

We all left for our assigned searches. Logan watched us buzz into a whirlwind of activity and followed me to the elevator. "I'll go with you, Audrey, because the Sky View deck has most of the bars."

# CHAPTER 64
### *Steve*

Carlee found Steve in their cabin sound asleep and gently snoring. The staff had tidied the room while they ate lunch, and Steve lay on top of the coverlet in his underwear with a blue and orange Boise State Broncos cap propped over his eyes. She noticed he had put on the new red bikini underwear she recently purchased for him. When he first saw them, he had growled, but later laughed as he modeled them for her. The front covered the necessities, and back side crossed his derriere with red strings but covered nothing. Carlee was instantly aroused at the sight of her used-to-be-very-sexy husband still looking sexier than other men. At seventy-eight years old, he was mostly fit and handsome, and she loved him and scolded herself for her impure thoughts about Griff. The bikini underwear clarified things for her.

"Steve. The captain is calling over the loudspeaker for a dentist. You have to get up, Steve, the captain wants a dentist," Carlee repeated loudly.

A sleepy, not-quite-awake Steve yawned and mumbled, "Huh? What? The captain wants sex? Is that what you said? How do you know he wants sex, and why are you waking me up?"

"No, Steve, he wants a dentist. He wants you."

"I'm not having sex with the captain and neither are you. Are you crazy? But you and I can have sex; that's a firecracker of an idea," Steve said as he pulled her down to the bed.

"You aren't listening, Steve. Something is wrong with the captain's tooth." She spoke directly into his ear, but it didn't help. Between his grogginess and his hearing, it seemed useless.

"We don't have any vermouth, but we can buy a bottle if you want," he cooed, nibbling her ears, one at a time as he unraveled her clothes from her body making her naked.

The announcement came over the loudspeaker one more time, no squeaking or squawking, loud and clear: *This is the captain speaking. Is there a dentist aboard? If you are a dentist, would you please contact the front desk?*

"Carlee, get off of me. The captain needs a dentist. Why didn't you tell me? You told me he wanted sex, but he wants a dentist." He jumped off the bed, adjusted his ball cap, and darted out the door, red bikinis ablaze.

Carlee threw on her clothes quickly to call him back when she heard a brief, but firm, rap at the door.

Carlee opened the door cautiously, and Steve stood in the hall with his hat on his head, "Carlee, I forgot something," he shouted, "my key card."

## CHAPTER 65
### *Steve*

Carlee snatched Steve's arm and yanked him inside the cabin, peeked around the door, looking both directions and breathing a sigh of relief that she didn't see anyone.

"What?" he exclaimed. "Give me my key card, that's all I need."

Carlee laughed out loud, "You need more than your key card, Hon, look at yourself in the mirror. Did anybody in the hall see you?"

Steve turned toward the mirror, and they both started to laugh. "I was so excited about the captain's tooth that I forgot I was mostly naked. Of course, I still have my hat on. While these red bikini drawers will liven up any party, I probably should throw shorts on." He turned and admired his backside with its four red strings crisscrossing it. "But I look good, don't I? Maybe I should do a few more sit-ups to flatten the tummy."

"You don't even do sit-ups, Steve. And you definitely look good, but we are not going to a bikini party, that's for sure. I bought the red bikini for you to parade around for me to ogle, not for the whole cruise ship. You are a spectacle to behold, but a cute one with a ridiculously cute butt. And sexy. Put your clothes on and you can fix the captain's tooth," Carlee laughed. "But, I'd better go with you."

Steve shifted his body to view himself from all sides, "If they have a bikini party, I'm sure as hell going. I look damn good for being seventy-eight years old. A few wrinkles here and there, but hell, I'm seventy-eight, and I've earned my wrinkles. My knees and hips don't ache, I don't have dementia, and I don't need adult diapers. I'm better off than many of our fellow passengers except for the fact that I can't hear. My wrinkles are badges of wisdom and maturity."

Carlee replied, "Possibly maturity but definitely not wisdom, especially if you want to parade around in those little panties in public because you might get arrested by the cruise police if there is such a thing. Did anybody see you when you traipsed through the hall?"

"I don't know. I didn't hear anything, but, hell, I can't hear anything anyway. I'm excited because this is the first time I've been needed since I retired. When I was a dentist, people needed me every day. People don't like dentists, even dread seeing them, but they need them, and the trouble with retirement is that no one needs you for anything. But today, the captain needs me."

"Let's get dressed and see about the captain's aching tooth," Carlee insisted. "I'll go with you."

"You still want Captain Morgan vermouth? They don't make it, Carlee, Martini and Rossi do. You can buy it on Amazon."

## CHAPTER 66
### *Steve*

Carlee and Steve arrived at the front desk fully clad and looking civilized. Steve still wore his Boise State Broncos cap, but trousers now hid his red bikini. "Where's the captain?" Steve asked the desk clerk. "I'm Dr. Sanderson, a dentist, and it seems the captain has a bad tooth, and I've come to fix it. I'm retired, but I kept my license to practice dentistry to be able to fix my kids' and grandkids' teeth. Carlee and I have eight kids and eighteen grandkids, and they all have teeth, except for the two who haven't been born yet."

The front desk clerk nodded, "I'll call the bridge and let the captain know you are here, but I didn't know the captain had a toothache."

"He has a bridge?" Steve asked. "Upper or lower? It's easier to work on a bridge than a back tooth without tools."

Steve sat down to wait for the captain of the ship, and Carlee looked around, "I'm going to order a glass of wine, but I'll be back in a few, I want to meet the captain, too."

"Ask if they have a bottle of Captain Morgan vermouth. You seem desperate for it," Steve called after her, "but they don't make it, Martini and Rossi does," he mumbled to himself.

"That's him! That's the guy who was naked in the hall, the pervert." A large blue-haired woman pointed at Steve and shouted. "He's the one. That one there." She had a shrill voice that carried throughout the lobby causing heads to turn.

"Murdered? Who's been murdered? What are you talking about?"

Steve worried aloud, not believing anyone could have been murdered on the ship.

The desk clerk picked up the phone and called security, as people began to slide away from Steve and his possible threats and others stepped closer to be part of the action. The throng created a buzz of murmurs, but Steve didn't hear any of it. Two uniformed security guards arrived within seconds to disperse the growing group. Steve looked around, wondering where the deceased was.

A uniformed man, who introduced himself as security officer Ricardo Rojas, approached the expanding group and asked, "What's going on? I received a call about a naked man with a red bikini and a hat on. Where is he?"

"That's him; he still has his hat on. He's dressed now, but he was running around naked in a red thong, which didn't cover much. He's the pervert," Virginia, the blue-haired lady accused before whispering to her friend, "but ooh la la, Sally, his thong was a sight to be seen. It was red with these little strings holding it together in the back. He has an extremely cute tush."

Officer Rojas asked the desk clerk, "Where's Dr. Sanderson, the dentist? I thought he was here."

The desk clerk pointed at Steve exclaiming, "That's him, that's Dr. Sanderson, but he's a pervert."

"I didn't murder anybody. I'm a dentist," Steve answered.

Carlee arrived with a large red drink with shrimp and vegetables hanging out of it, and approached Steve and others, "Steve, what did you do?"

"Nothing, they keep saying I murdered a person, but I didn't. I'm a dentist. You tell them, Carlee."

"No, Steve, they don't think you are a murderer, they think you are a pervert. Somebody must have seen you in the hall when you forgot your clothes," Carlee told him. "It's all a big mix-up, and we need to explain."

"I'm not a pervert, I'm a dentist. I fix teeth. You tell them, Carlee," Steve repeated.

Two more badged people arrived, and the three security guards accompanied Steve and Carlee into a small office adjacent to the front desk. Officer Rojas asked, "Were you in the hall naked? That's not acceptable, Dr. Sanderson. You are Dr. Sanderson, aren't you?"

Carlee took over the conversation explaining about Steve losing his hearing aids and being unable to hear and how he became excited at being asked to help the captain with his decayed tooth and forgot he was nearly naked and accidently went into the hall. Officer Rojas listened and nodded and answered, "Okay" or "Right" a few times before saying, "Okay, but for right now we have a situation requiring tooth repair, and we need a dentist. Thank you for answering our summons." Rojas dismissed the security guards to calm Virginia, the blue-haired lady, and her friend Sally.

Steve tried to take the conversation back in hand, "As I started to say, I'm retired, but I'm still a dentist. Where's the captain? I thought he needed a dentist."

Officer Rojas responded, "It's not the captain, but someone on board who needs a dentist. The tooth probably has to be pulled because it's cracked wide open."

"I can pull the tooth, but I need to look at it first before deciding what to do. I don't have any tools but will see how the medical department can assist me. I might need an antibiotic for infection and anesthetic to numb the pain, but I'll figure it out. Where's the patient?" Steve asked.

"I'll take you to him, his name is Jack."

## CHAPTER 67
### *Gus*

"It's time for a trial run, Gus," Dr. Lewis said after she had taken his vital signs, poked and prodded, and examined him from head to toe. He had undressed for her for the second day in a row and now sat on the gurney with a towel wrapped around his midriff, leaving his backside stranded. He felt a little nervous about rocking and rolling with Dr. Lewis. He liked her, but she was a doctor, maybe beyond his station in life. She was fifty-something with a medical degree from Harvard, and he was a nearly seventy-year-old retired physical education teacher from Hunter, and they didn't quite match. And he loved Phyllis.

He and Phyllis celebrated their retirements and their fortieth wedding anniversary with a cruise to Hawaii last summer and had renewed their marriage vows on the ship promising each other to try for another forty years. Yet, here he was, ogling the lusty and busty Dr. Lewis. He knew Phyllis would never stray, but his lifetime of fantasies about guilty pleasures and forbidden fruit had rattled his brain for years, and now, here she was: Dr. Vivian Lewis, Doctor of Medicine. Sexy and available. And better still, she wanted him.

She had smooth brown skin and an enticing smile. Her teeth gleamed white and her brown eyes half closed when she looked at him, considering them sexy and perhaps even an invitation for a frisky frolic. She wore her curly black hair off her neck with wispy strands that tickled her ears.

Gus found women of physical substance more desirable than those bony women whose meat barely clung to their skeletons. The skinnies were all right, but they reminded him of the scrawny acne-covered teenagers who had filled his physical education classes through the years. Piles of soft flesh gave him more pleasure and made his love sausage a little livelier. The jiggle and waggle of Phyllis' extra flesh grew sexier over the years. In his mind, she had the perfect body, in fact, if anything, he wouldn't object if she gained a few more pounds. More flesh to fondle would make her even spicier.

Dr. Lewis was right, Gus topped three-hundred pounds, but had a little ass that she thought adorable. Dr. Lewis, no skinny mini herself with large sexy boobs, owned a fantastic ass rounding her out nicely. He appreciated her shape and her energy and loved her plain talk about his health and her horniness. He looked at the gurney and sighed, "No way we'll fit on the gurney because it's too narrow for our ample bodies. I barely fit on it alone, and we might droop over the edges, but what do you have in mind? Your place or mine?"

"Never fear, Gus, my dear, Dr. Lewis is here, and I'm all over it," she answered, rolling out a second gurney from the closet. She grabbed a roll of heavy-duty adhesive tape and taped the two together and threw a set of sheets on the makeshift lovemaking nest. "You've been on my mind since you rolled into my clinic last weekend, and I finally found the nerve to ask the housekeeping staff for extra linen, and it's all ready. I didn't know if you felt the same as me, a little horny, a little eager, but now clean sheets, a do-not-disturb sign on the door, and we're ready for some monkey business. Lucky for you I had early menopause, meaning we don't have to worry about any little Gus'."

She took his temperature and checked his pulse, pulled out her stethoscope and checked his heart. "You're good to go, Gus, let's get it on," exclaimed Dr. Vivian Lewis, Doctor of Monkey Business.

Dr. Lewis and Gus had no trouble *getting it on* as she had called their earlier activity. After the panic attack, she had ordered him *not to shoot the moon with your beautiful bride*, and now he was shooting the moon with the one who forbade him to shoot the moon. He and Phyllis had not had any meaningful sex since he retired five years ago, even though he had told a different story to Griff.

"This gurney is damn hard," Gus grumbled to Dr. Lewis, "and the side rail is a killer. It's poking me in the ass. We should have gone to a cabin. Mine or yours."

"That's only because you have such a dinky ass. You won't find me complaining about my ample ass because it means more cushion for my pushin', if you get my drift," Dr. Lewis teased, rolling on top of him, eager for round two.

Dinky ass or not, the weight of two oversized torsos on the gurney was too much and it collapsed with a thunderous, metallic crash, and the two of them plummeted to the floor with the second, taped gurney askew, anchoring them to each other. Dr. Lewis looked at Gus and laughed aloud, "Well, that was the ultimate climax."

Gus, lying beneath her, could see a tag listing the gurney's particulars dangling from the side rails. "We need to recalibrate, Doc. This gurney has a weight limit of three hundred pounds."

"I know, that's why I taped two together, six hundred pounds." She paused, "Oops. We were both on one."

## CHAPTER 68
### *Jack Black*

The first officer escorted Steve to Mel Black's cabin with Carlee trailing behind. "Does Jack have a last name?" Steve asked.

"Brown or maybe Black, or maybe he doesn't have one, I'm not sure," Officer Rojas replied. "I don't know much about him, other than he needs a dentist."

They arrived at the cabin, and Mel opened the door. "I know you," Steve greeted, "you're the guy with the seeing eye dog. I've seen you around the ship a few times."

Mel didn't comment, but asked a question, "Are you a dentist?"

"Yes, I'm a dentist, but I don't have any tools on board. I'm retired but have my license, so don't worry, I can help Jack. Did he hurt the tooth or did the pain come on suddenly or gradually?" Steve asked Mel.

Mel answered, "He hurt himself on the sled ride in Funchal when he jumped out of the toboggan and banged his face on the concrete wall. I had tied him up, but he leaped out anyway and now he has a broken tooth that probably needs to come out. His gums have icky stuff coming out of them. I can't see it, but it oozes like cottage cheese, all gooey. Plus, he winces when I touch them."

Carlee looked at him in horror, "Why was he tied up? If he was scared, you shouldn't have taken him. That was terrible. Did he hurt anything else? I mean, break anything? You probably should have him checked by a neurologist to be sure he didn't get a concussion. We didn't go on the sled ride, but we heard it was scary."

Steve reassured him, "Even without tools, I can help you enough to get by for a few days until you get home and can see your own dentist. I'll get a pain reliever and antibiotics from the clinic and hopefully ward off any infection. Where is Jack?"

"He's lying down because he doesn't have enough energy to get up and move. The hurt tooth is one of his upper pointy front teeth. He'll be glad to see you," Mel continued. "He hasn't eaten because it's too painful. I gave him a bowl of water, but he hasn't touched it either. He's twelve and getting old, but I'm no good without him."

"Twelve isn't old, he's a kid. Let me see him," Steve insisted, "Where is he?"

"He's lying down on the bathroom floor by the toilet because that's where he prefers to sleep. I put the bathmat on the floor to make it a little softer and more comfortable," Mel explained. "Don't worry, he won't bite you even though he's in pain."

Carlee was appalled, "Did you say he sleeps on the bathroom floor? I can't believe you would tie up your twelve-year-old son and let him sleep on the bathroom floor. If my child slept on the floor, he might bite, too. What kind of father are you?"

"My son?" Mel laughed, "No, you have it wrong, Jack is my dog."

## CHAPTER 69
### *Jack Black*

Steve stared at Mel asking, "Jack in a box? I don't understand."
Carlee answered him, "No, Jack's not in a box; he's in the bathroom
and is a dog. D-O-G, you know, chasing cars and barking," adding, "woof-
woof, like Daisy."

Steve asked Mel, "Oh, a dog. Your dog broke his tooth? Not you? Not
your son?"

Carlee took a deep breath, "That's better, I thought you were talking
about tying up your son who fell out of the toboggan and slept on the
floor."

Steve shook his head, "I don't know, I've never done dental work on a
dog. I have a dog, Daisy, but she's never had a cavity that I know of. Show
me where he is, and I'll have a look."

Jack faced the door and rested his head on a wad of towels. He looked
up and gave out an anemic sound, half growl and half bark, as Steve
entered the tiny bathroom. A large driblet of festering goo had dripped
onto the towel matting it into this chin and lower jowls.

Steve leaned down, "Okay, Jack, I want to look at your tooth," Jack
dropped his head back down on the towels and closed his eyes. "This is
not going to work because I need to be able to see his tooth. It's his upper
tooth and I can't see anything from here. Let me get down on the floor.
Give me a hand, will you, Carlee?"

As Carlee stretched over to offer him support, her Bloody Mary
slipped from her hand onto the floor. The plastic footed glass didn't break,

but the contents, including the salad makings and shrimp splattered everywhere, on Steve, Mel, and Jack, bringing an anguished yelp from Jack. Steve tried to kneel, but his knee gave out when he bent over, and he slammed to the floor, missing the dog but spilling Jack's bowl of water. He landed on his backside with his feet splayed to his front and he cried out. "Dammit, I hope I didn't injure my hip."

Steve ignored his water-and-tomato-juice-soaked pants and lay prone beside Jack attempting to pry Jack's mouth open, but Jack was in no mood to cooperate, doing his anemic bark/growl again. "He's not going to bite me, is he, Mel?"

"He's a service dog and has been trained not to bite, but he's in a great deal of pain, so I'm not sure what he will or won't do. He's never bitten anyone before but there is always a first time. You should be fine if you don't hurt him."

"Can you move him to the bed?" Carlee suggested. "Steve would have a better chance at seeing his tooth."

"I'll try, but I'm not sure he will cooperate. Plus, he's a full-sized dog and will be a dead weight to lift," Mel added.

Mel pushed Jack away from the toilet to get a firm grasp to hoist him into his arms, but Jack wasn't having any part of it and emitted a painful yelp followed by a frightened snarl and braced himself to stay where he was.

Steve gave it another go, but Jack's lips were stuck together, and he responded the same as before. "Another option is to sedate him before moving him to the bed, where I can work on him. Or perhaps Dr. Lewis would allow us to use the clinic, and I could extract the tooth while he's sedated. Actually, the clinic might be the better choice. It would be easier to work on him."

"I agree," Mel said, "will the clinic give you a sedation drug?"

"Dr. Lewis probably might, but sedating Jack will be different from human patients. How much does he weigh?"

"About eighty pounds."

Carlee said, "Let's go, Steve, the clinic is open now. Do you have your medical ID card? You might need it."

Once at the clinic, Steve recited Jack's situation and their plan to the LPN at the reception desk, but she referred him to Dr. Lewis to get the drug. "She's in the last exam room with a patient, second door around the corner on the right. You can wait for her outside the room."

Carlee and Steve retreated and found chairs to sit in. They waited several minutes and suddenly heard a crash, thud, moaning, and an umph. Carlee, ever the curious one, ignored the DND sign and cracked the door to the exam room to peek in. "Gus. Dr. Lewis. Whatever are you doing?" Gus, naked as nothing, struggled to free himself from under an equally bare-assed Dr. Lewis. Gus' eyes opened full circle, and he sputtered unintelligibly, while Dr. Lewis howled with laughter.

## CHAPTER 70
### Audrey

Logan and I had searched all the bars but didn't see Steve. I wondered aloud, "Surely Carlee has located Steve by now, since we haven't heard any more announcements about needing a dentist. I want to see what has happened to Griff. Since he wasn't in any of the bars, maybe he's by the pool or in the cafeteria."

"We can wander around a bit, hit the cafeteria and the pool, and then enjoy some ice cream with a dollop of whipped cream. He'll probably show up if we eat enough ice cream. We've only gone through about fifteen gallons today, meaning we have another couple hundred to go," Logan chuckled.

Phyllis was halfway through a hot chocolate sundae with whipped cream when we arrived. "I looked all over the casino and coffee shops but couldn't find Steve. I thought I would take a break and maybe he would come by here. This sundae is so delicious, I just might have another. Did you find Steve? Or did Carlee?"

"We don't know whether Carlee found him or not, but we didn't," Logan told her, "and we had the same idea as you, eat ice cream until he walked by. "I'll order. Do you want the usual?"

\*\*\*

"Isn't Logan a gentleman? He seems nice, but I haven't talked with him very much. I'd like to get to know him better," Phyllis told me, fingering her bracelet. "I could complain of a foot or toe disease if I knew the symptoms, but since he keeps his eyes glued to you, it probably wouldn't matter. Do you two have something going?"

Logan was tempting and certainly was making a play for me, but I was trying to remain loyal to Griff. I answered, "Logan? Oh, no, we're friends, that's all. He doesn't know anybody on the cruise, and he seems lonely. We both are fond of ice cream even though we are trying to live healthy. He's easy to talk to, and I've learned a lot about feet. He's still grieving for his wife, Joan."

Logan brought two bowls of ice cream and sat down at the round metal table. He had a separate bowl of whipped cream, *Just in case of emergency*, he declared.

Phyllis looked puzzled, "Just in case what? I've can't say I have ever heard of a whipped cream emergency. Whipped cream is one of my favorite foods because it is sensuous, lusty, and delicious, almost sassy, all the same words you can use to describe sex, but I've never known it to be part of an emergency."

"He's a big tease," I explained. "He just chatters about whipped cream because he loves sundaes."

Griff walked in, saying, "I wondered where everybody was. I've been all over the ship and couldn't find any of you. I even checked at the med center, concerned Gus might have been sick again. Doc, you haven't forgotten about my bunion, have you? It's hurting badly, but right now, Audrey, I want to go to the free wine-tasting class that starts in a few minutes, and since it's on this deck, we don't have far to go."

"Why don't we have a look at your bunion right now?" Logan offered, with a cunning grin on his face.

## CHAPTER 71
### *Steve*

"**O**ut!" Dr. Lewis ordered, "Carlee, get out! Can't you see I'm examining a patient? You have to leave now."

Gus' saucer eyes stared, and he beamed red in a flash. "Oh, Carlee, don't tell Phyllis. Please. She won't understand." He unsuccessfully struggled to free himself from beneath Dr. Lewis, searching for a towel or sheet to cover himself.

Carlee was grinning from ear to ear, "Oh, yeah. Doc, I see you have given Gus an A to Z full body exam, but don't worry, it will be our little secret. Don't worry about a thing, Gus. This is the icing on my birthday cake!" She laughed out loud at seeing them on the floor under the gurney.

Steve saw the entwined pair on the floor, but ignored the situation, "Dr. Lewis, I need drugs for Jack. Could you give me what I need? I need them right away."

"Who's Jack?" Dr. Lewis asked as she started to get off the floor, still bare from top to bottom. She grabbed a sheet off the toppled gurney and wrapped it around her torso and tossed Gus a washcloth, concealing little.

"Jack broke his tooth when he jumped out of the toboggan and hit it on a cement wall in Funchal. It's a bad break and needs to come out," Steve said.

"Jack who?" Dr. Lewis repeated.

"Jack Black," Carlee answered. "He's a black Labrador with a broken tooth."

Dr. Lewis was puzzled and getting a little hot, "I don't care where he's from or what race he is, and I haven't heard about anybody getting hurt in Funchal. I have no idea what you are talking about. If he broke a tooth, he probably needs to see a dentist. Now get out."

"I am a dentist," Steve retorted. "Retired, but licensed, and I need drugs."

"Leave, both of you, before I call security," Dr. Lewis shouted shoving Carlee out of the way to slam the door.

Steve didn't budge, "What celebrity? Why would you want a celebrity?"

Carlee shook her head, "No, Steve, security. They already called security on you once for being a pervert, and we don't want security again. They think you're a pervert and might lock you up for trying to get drugs."

"But I need drugs, Carlee, if I'm going to help Jack," he repeated.

Dr. Lewis responded, "Well, I could vouch for you being a pervert. You busted into my exam room while I'm examining poor Gus, trying my best to keep him from having another panic attack. You keep demanding that I give you drugs. Now, get out, you drug addicted pervert."

# CHAPTER 72
## *Griff*

We had finished our ice cream, and Logan suggested to Griff, "Let's go out on the deck, and I'll take a look at your bunion. It will be lighter up there, and I will be able to see it better. They can be painful, and there are only a few remedies, but maybe I can conjure up a treatment."

"It's about time," Griff grumbled, "I've been suffering with this bunion for a few months, but my GP won't touch it. He advised me to see a specialist, but this cruise came up, and it's getting worse. It's grown bigger and redder and now hurts like hell. I hope you can fix it."

Griff, Logan, and I moved to the pool area, leaving Phyllis behind. The chilly weather discouraged people from swimming or hot tubbing, but Charlie "the Bird" Parker sat by the edge of the pool and hopped toward us. Griff took off his sandals and sat down on a lounge chair and extended his leg, so Logan could see his foot. "Here you go, Doc, my fine-looking bunion is right there."

The purplish-red bunion had disfigured Griff's big toe, sliding it toward the other toes. It looked painful, and Griff winced when Logan took Griff's foot in his hand and pushed and prodded his big toe and agreed, "Yes, indeed, you have a fine-looking bunion, but I might have a remedy. I could do surgery, but, of course, I can't cut on the ship. Another choice is to alternate icing and heating it: ice-heat-ice-heat. You get the picture? That will tie you down, and you'd have to do it constantly for a few weeks. Or you can wear a splint, the most effective method of treatment. I have splints in my medical bag because you never know when you'll need a bunion splint."

"A bunion splint? I've never heard of it. Does it hurt? What does it look like?" Griff asked.

Logan placed his hands on Griff's foot to explain the product, "The splint I have is made of white plastic with cloth straps and attaches to your foot with Velcro across the arch, and loops around the heel to the big toe. It has a little air pump to adjust the pressure on the bunion. The more pressure you apply, the faster the bunion will go away and, in a few weeks, wham, shazam, thank you ma'am, it nearly disappears. I say nearly because it could pop up later. When you get home, you should see a podiatrist, and he or she might be able to fit you in a boot with air pressure. I've seen good results with those, but I didn't bring a bunion boot with me."

"A few weeks? Do I have to use the splint at night, too? Will it affect our three-a-days?" Griff wanted to know.

"It might be a turn off, I don't know. No one has ever asked me that question before," Logan responded. "You put it on your foot and then put your shoe on. It's easy to do and these sandals are perfect. I recommend you rest your foot for the first few days you use the splint, put your foot up, and increase the pressure to improve its success. While aboard the ship, you could spend time on your balcony and read a book. What do you say, Griff, do you want to try it?"

"Sure, Doc, I'll try it, even though that means I have to spend the rest of the cruise in my cabin. That's a bummer, I enjoy dancing with Audrey, but I guess I have danced my last dance, at least for right now." Griff looked at me and shrugged, "I know you're disappointed, Hon, but I've gotta do something. The pain has become almost unbearable."

I nodded, "Well, yes, your toe is most important."

"I'll get the splint to put on your foot. Stay right here," Logan advised Griff.

Curious about the activity around Griff, Charlie Parker flew to the lounge chair and looked at the foot, pecking at it with his bill. "Hey, quit that," Griff scolded the bird and nudged him away with his other foot. Go away, Charlie. Go bother somebody else."

A few minutes later Logan returned with the splint and applied it to Griff's foot. He started to pick up Griff's sandals, but didn't. "Charlie Parker seems to be cranky with you, Griff, he left you a slimy white present in your sandals."

"Oh, shit," Griff said.

"That's exactly what it is, Griff," Logan agreed, chuckling.

## CHAPTER 73
### *Steve*

Gus lay on the floor and rolled over trying to get up, groaning and grunting as he pushed himself to his knees. "Dammit," Gus moaned, "I banged my back when the gurney collapsed, and I might need a hand getting up, Doc. There is no way Carlee will keep this a secret. She'll tell everybody, Phyllis, Griff, Audrey. Maybe even the foot guy. Steve saw us but didn't seem to take notice of my lying naked on the floor; he was too busy begging for drugs."

"Here you go, Honey, let me help you up," Dr. Lewis offered. "You were right, we should have gone to my cabin. That's what we'll do next time."

Gus shrieked, "Next time? There won't be a next time because Phyllis will kill me when Carlee tells her, and she'll feed me to the sharks. She would never cheat on me and now...oh, man, what do I do?"

"Oh, Gus. Settle down. Steve didn't notice, and it will be Carlee's word against mine because I'm a doctor, treating my patient, and that's what we'll say. I loved our little gurney ride. You are a great lover; Phyllis is one lucky woman," Dr. Lewis smiled as she gazed at Gus. She moved toward him and kissed him gently. "I have no regrets."

They dressed and put the exam room back together including disassembling their makeshift hideaway. Dr. Lewis checked his heart rate again with her stethoscope and repeated her suggestion of losing a few pounds before sending him out the door. "Same time tomorrow, Gus."

"Will we...," his voice trailed off. "I hope so." He leaned forward and kissed her.

Gus cracked open the door, horrified to see Steve sitting in a chair outside the exam room. Steve stood up and asked Gus, "Is she still in there? Tell her I need drugs for Jack's tooth."

"Who is Jack?" Gus asked, scanning the hall, afraid of seeing Carlee or even worse, Phyllis. He closed the exam room door behind him asking, "Where's Carlee?"

"Carlee is looking for a drink. Jack is Mel's dog, and he has a broken tooth. I need to pull it out before it gets further infected," Steve informed Gus.

Gus was a little confused, "Mel has a broken tooth?"

"No, Jack, the seeing eye dog. Where is Dr. Lewis? I need to see her," Steve repeated.

Dr. Lewis opened the door to the hall. "Are you still here? I told you no drugs."

"They aren't for me, Doc, they are for Jack, the seeing eye dog. He broke his tooth when he jumped out of the toboggan, and he's pretty sick. His mouth is infected, and his tooth needs to be extracted."

She peered at him suspiciously, "Oh, I get it now. Jack is the black Labrador. I thought you meant a person from Labrador, you know, a Canadian. I didn't know the dog fell out of the toboggan. I didn't even know we had a seeing-eye dog on board the ship. What do you need?"

"His tooth needs to come out, and I need an anesthetic, an antibiotic, and a place to do the surgery. Right now, he's lying on the floor by the toilet in Mel's cabin, and I can't lie on the floor to extract his tooth," Steve explained.

Dr. Lewis nodded in agreement, "That might be tough, so why don't we put him on a gurney and bring him to the clinic? We have an extra exam room, and I have instruments and antibiotics you can use."

"He needs to be sedated in order to put him on the gurney because he's distressed, and he might bite me," Steve replied with urgency in his voice.

Dr. Lewis unlocked a cabinet and removed a vial and a syringe. "Let's go. Gus, you come, too, because we might need help lifting the dog to the gurney. She wheeled a gurney back into the exam room, and Steve began pushing it. She whispered to Gus, "This gurney is getting a great workout today."

When they arrived at Mel's room, Dr. Lewis injected Jack with a drug that sedated him within a minute, and Gus and Mel carefully lifted him onto the gurney. Dr. Lewis concealed him completely with a sheet, hiding him from view of the public. "That might raise eyebrows," she explained.

Steve pushed the gurney toward the elevator with Gus, Mel, and Dr. Lewis following. The elevator doors slid open, and the lady with the blue hair and her friend exited, "Oh, my God, it's the pervert. Now what has he done, murdered somebody?"

## CHAPTER 74
### *Steve*

"How's Jack?" Mel asked, when Steve and Dr. Lewis came out of the examination room after extracting the dog's canine tooth. Gus and Carlee were waiting with Mel as Gus munched on carrot sticks and Carlee sipped a drink with an umbrella.

Steve held the tooth up for everyone to see. The tooth was long and a little bloody, but it was obvious that Steve was proud of his work. "Piece of cake," Steve bragged, "Jack was a good patient, but he hasn't come out of the anesthetic yet. Dr. Lewis anesthetized him, and she did a bang-up job. He'll be fine. His mouth will be sore for a few days, and you should feed him soft food, maybe mash up the dog food. He might look a little lopsided with only one long canine, but he'll be a good service dog for you. Not having dental tools made it more difficult, but he'll be fine. Do you want the tooth? It's cracked but I extracted it in one piece, not in chunks. You could put it on a chain and make it into a necklace." Steve put the tooth in Mel's hand.

"Lopsided," Mel wanted to know. "How could he be lopsided? Is he limping or something? I don't care if he's lopsided, but could you wrap the tooth in plastic, so I can decide what to do with it later? And what's the slick, goopy stuff, blood?"

Steve answered, "The goopy stuff on the tooth is just dog saliva, you know, spit. Don't worry, it'll dry."

Dr. Lewis patted Mel on the back, giving accolades to Steve, "You were lucky Dr. Steve came on this cruise because I could never have done what he did. Jack was a good patient, and he'll come out of the anesthesia within a few minutes, but you should take him down to your room on the gurney before he wakes up because he'll be in no condition to walk far and he might argue about riding on the gurney. Mel, Carlee, and Steve, you three take him back to his cabin. Gus, you stay here and help me clean up the exam room. Many guests would not understand treating a dog in a people's clinic. You know, appearances, so be sure to keep Jack covered up, head to toe. Those two ladies we met by the elevator accused Steve of having a dead body, and we don't want them telling people we have multiple bodies. The clinic reopens in half an hour, so we've gotta move fast."

Mel, Steve, and Carlee obeyed her and wheeled the gurney out the door to the elevator. Gus and Dr. Lewis headed back into the exam room to ready it for human patients, but Dr. Lewis bypassed the exam room and entered her private office and before long, she nudged Gus toward the couch.

"What about cleaning up the exam room?" Gus asked, "you know, making it fit for humans?"

"We'll throw the sheets in the laundry and the nighttime cleaning staff will wipe everything else down, like they do every night. It is an extra exam room that doesn't get used that often, so it is okay to leave it for now. Don't worry, Gus, we just have to be out of my office by the time Carlee and Steve bring back the gurney."

## CHAPTER 75
### *Audrey*

When Griff and I awoke two mornings before docking in Lisbon, an envelope had been shoved under the door. Griff had on his bunion splint and little else, and he found it difficult to move, let alone walk, and asked me to retrieve the envelope. He had pumped the splint as tightly as he could tolerate and had become as cranky as a crone with a splinter in her vagina.

He sat on the edge of the bed grumbling about not doing the dirty because the splint had scratched my foot forcing me to sleep on the couch, which I was glad to do. He stood up, nearly tripped on the air pump, and let loose with a few swear words, "I hate this thing. I doubt it will even work, and I'm starting to think he's a quack."

I picked up the envelope and held it up for him to see, "Patience, Grasshopper," I said. "Logan told you it might take a few weeks, and you need to be patient. This envelope must contain a summary of our bill. Carlee and Phyllis' statements arrived yesterday, but Logan hadn't gotten his. Do you want to open it, or do you want me to open it before throwing myself off the balcony when I see how much we frittered away?"

"I'd better open it because I don't want you jumping overboard, because who would wait on me then?" Griff answered. "We probably spent $1,000 maybe $1,500 with the suite, the clothes, the drinks, and excursions. The cruise was listed at $1,500 each for ten days...plus taxes, port fees and all the other fees they tack on. I already paid three grand."

I started tapping out a drum roll on the arm of the couch. "Go for it.

Let's check to see how many soybeans we spent."

"I could make a better guess if you had asked how much more the suite would cost," he reminded me.

"Your words: *no matter what,* which meant to me it didn't matter. I'm glad we had a suite though, aren't you? Did you see any of the other rooms, I mean, Steve or Gus' rooms? Or Logan's? They are okay and cost less than this one, but I appreciated having this luxurious suite for our inaugural cruise, and I am now officially spoiled," I noted.

"You've been spoiled since the day we met and more so since I retired. What other woman gets the big O several times a day?" Griff teased, as he wound his hips in a circle saying in a falsetto voice, "Oh, Griff, don't stop, please don't stop," he continued, mocking an orgasm. "Okay, here it goes, start the drum roll, again…the envelope, please, and the charge to our paper-thin credit card is, what? $7,800? That can't be right. I might throw us both off the balcony. How much did the suite cost?"

"You must be kidding. $7,800? How much did the suite cost?" I echoed, instantly regretting spending so much money.

"It says here $5,000 but it doesn't say anything about the three thousand bucks we already paid. This has to be a mistake. If it's not a mistake, this little 10-day cruise cost us one thousand bucks a day, and I had planned on $150 a day. That's a lot of soybeans, Audrey, a lot of damn soybeans."

"We should take the bill down to the front desk and ask for an itemized statement," I suggested.

"They have the list right here. The biggest cost, besides the suite, was a dress. It must be the hot red dress you wore to the gala. That little number was $450. I will say that even though it cost the big bucks, it was worth every cent because you were the hottest babe around. Logan thought so, too. All the men stared at you. By the way, you and Logan aren't doing anything behind old Griffy's jingle-berries are you? His eyes are all over you, but he is working on my bunion for free, which I appreciate, and I'd hate to have to kill him."

"No, your jingle has done its last jangle, at least until the bunion gets better," I answered, glad he hadn't asked about Logan's intention. I loved the attention Logan had bestowed on me, but those wedding vows echoed in my head. The bunion splint had put a damper on Griff's enthusiasm, and I had wondered more than once if jingling Logan's jingle-berries, would be the same as with Griff.

I was thinking of Logan, but Griff had his mind on the bill, wondering how it had gotten out of control. "Did you buy the tuxedo and all the stuff going with it? Renting it would have been cheaper, but this says you bought it, and it cost another $400. I looked good though, didn't I? Other than those two costly items, everything else was for drinks. There's a pair of earrings, but they cost about $100…not too bad, and the wild ride in the toboggan cost $200."

"Yeah, you looked good. I bought the tux because I am planning another cruise, and you'll have to have a tuxedo for that trip, too," I reminded him.

Griff smiled, "Yes, we should go again, but where do you want to go next time? I wouldn't mind, but let's go to a place where we can bask in the sun, maybe Aruba with lots of coastline where we can get naked and have sex on the beach."

"Not unless you get rid of your bunion," I said emphatically.

## CHAPTER 76
### Audrey

I left Griff on the balcony resting his bunion while I visited the front desk to verify our credit card charges. *Yes, it was expensive, but this had been the most fun I had had since I retired. Griff had asked me several times about Logan, whether we were doing the dirty. We weren't, but it wasn't like Logan hadn't tried, and I had considered it more than once and nixed it, God knows why. If Griff knew how much fun I had, he would be thrilled. If Griff knew what fun I wanted, I would be killed.*

A long queue of guests waited in the reception area, everyone holding an envelope in their hands. *Lots of questions*, I thought, *others must be questioning whether their charges exceeded the expected amount as well.*

"Good morning, Miss Audrey," a voice murmured over my shoulder. "It seems many guests have questions concerning their charges or are making new reservations or are checking flights home. What are you doing here? Waiting for me, I hope."

I looked behind me and greeted Logan who was smiling a slightly crooked smile. My upper and lower parts were jingling, as Griff said. Logan's presence continued to make everything fidget and awkwardness set in, like rain on a cloudy day. "Yes, I wasn't exactly waiting for you, in the sense of waiting, but I knew you would appear, which is nice. Griff questioned the cost of the suite but everything else is okay. He initially paid for the room on the third deck, and he's concerned about double charges. I'm sure everything is fine, but I'll verify the charges to make him happy. As you predicted, the bunion splint has made him as grouchy as a mama moose with twin calves."

"What's on your agenda today, your next to last day on the ship? Does anything include me? May I give you a toe massage or offer you another type of toe pleasure?" he asked innocently.

I sighed, "Yes, no, maybe…well, yes, I do need help, you know, the blisters and other maladies I have acquired on this trip. I'd never refuse a free podiatry exam."

Logan perked up at my *yes, no, maybe* and said, "You have more to worry about than your blisters, you know. The thing is, I noticed an irregularity of your feet when I examined them earlier, and I want to recheck, if that's okay with you."

"What about my feet? Do you see a problem with my foot? I don't have athlete's foot or hammer toe, do I?" I pretended alarm.

"No, what's wrong with your feet is that they drive me crazy, and I want reexamine them closely to discover the source of my being so turned on every time you are in the vicinity," Logan said. "By the way, how is Griff's bunion coming along? Any progress?"

"I don't know, he threatens to kill you on a regular basis, but other than that, he's normal," I giggled. "I keep reminding him you aren't charging him for your services."

"Tonight's another gala night. Will Griff be up for it? If not, would you let me escort you?" Logan did a little bow, "It would be my pleasure, Miss Audrey, and I promise to behave myself, despite the fact my libido goes into overdrive when you are around."

I shook my head, "Oh, dear, I forgot about the gala tonight, and I don't want to wear the same dress twice, so between his bunion and my lack of a dress, we'll have to forego the gala. He can't possibly put his formal shoes on over the bunion splint."

"Lack of a dress sounds delightful," he teased, "but you would never go for that. What about the black one you talked about earlier? The one that was backless and armless and frontless or whatever. It sounds amazing, and it would please me to buy it for you, if you will allow me. I loved to buy dresses and jewelry for Joan, but now she is gone, and I would be honored to buy it for you. After you straighten out your charges, let's grab a bite to eat and check the shops to see if the black dress is still available."

I finally moved to the front of the line and confirmed my bill to be correct. The room had cost $8,000, $3,000 Griff had paid previously and $5,000 additional for the suite, plus $2,800 for miscellaneous charges. Plus, maybe another gown. Everything was correct.

# CHAPTER 77
*Carlee*

J ack snored softly, asleep on Mel's bed, when Steve and Carlee left. Mel
thanked Steve profusely, and offered to pay him, but for Steve, just being
needed was reward enough, and he refused to take any money for his
services. It had been a long time since he had helped anyone, albeit a dog.

Extracting Jack's canine had worn Steve out, tiring him more than he
thought it would. While Steve returned to their cabin for a well-deserved
nap, Carlee volunteered to take the gurney to the medical clinic located
on the first deck. Mel's room was on the sixth, and the elevator did not
appear to be in any hurry. It stopped at each floor to let people on or off,
most of whom she had never seen before. *How can that be,* she wondered,
*ten days on a cruise and I'm still seeing new folks.* Most were curious about
the now-empty gurney, but she only hinted at the subject and his medical
needs, citing HIPAA rules, but said he was doing fine.

At last, she and the gurney arrived, and exited the elevator, facing
a new group of people waiting to see a doctor or nurse in the medical
clinic. They badgered her with questions about the gurney until finally
the LPN rescued her and led her to the back of the clinic to help her store
the gurney in a closet. "Where's Dr. Lewis?" she asked the LPN. "Could I
see her?"

"Not now, because she's in her office with a patient, but she'll be out
soon. You are welcome to wait if you'd like. Most of these people only
need prescriptions refilled or their blood pressure taken. Most don't need
to see Dr. Lewis," the LPN assured her.

"I wanted to thank her for helping Steve. This was the best thing that's happened to him in a long time, and I want to say thanks," Carlee explained.

"I'll tell her," the LPN offered.

"I'll wait," Carlee replied contemplating who her patient might be. *Gus?* A few minutes later, the door to Dr. Lewis' office swung open and out came red-faced Gus with his uncombed combover sticking out in several directions. He seemed short-winded and walked slowly, halfway between waddling and shuffling, "Gus, what's wrong? You look like you don't feel well. Where's Phyllis? Do you want me to find Phyllis?" Carlee offered with an unsure smile on her face.

"No, Carlee, no Phyllis. I've had a panic attack relapse, and Dr. Lewis worked me through it, but I don't want to worry Phyllis, so please keep it to yourself. HIPAA and all that."

He looked terrible, and Carlee thought he might be telling the truth. She didn't want to cause him any more stress or grief, so she agreed, "All right Gus, I won't mention anything to her but take care of yourself."

Gus continued out the door, and moments later, Dr. Lewis exited her office, donning her white coat and draping her stethoscope around her neck as she noted Carlee. She looked a little discombobulated with uncombed hair and her unsmoothed skirt lying crooked with the top two buttons of her blouse unfastened. Carlee had second thoughts about whether Gus had told the truth. She greeted Dr. Lewis who immediately asked about Jack and his tooth and if Steve had survived the tooth extraction himself.

## CHAPTER 78
### *Audrey*

Logan and I headed to the Broadway for breakfast and ordered our meals. He offered again, "I'm serious about buying you that dress. I want to do it for you. You must know I'm crazy about you, and unfortunately for me, you refuse to accept my advances, so, please, at least let me buy you a dress."

I shook my head again. He is so persistent. "You don't have to buy the dress, Logan, because I am perfectly capable of buying my own clothes."

"That could be true, but I'll accompany you to buy it because I'd like to see it on you. Or off you. Either way," he flirted. "I haven't bought a dress in a long time, and it's time I did," he laughed. "Joan would be proud of me, and I think she would enjoy you."

We were finishing our waffles when Phyllis and Gus joined us for breakfast, followed by Steve and Carlee moments later. Soon the table was filled with plates and cups of coffee and chatter. "Where's Griff?" Carlee asked, "He isn't sick, is he?"

"No, it's his bunion. Logan put a bunion splint on it to reduce the pain, and now he has to stay in the room," I explained.

Phyllis suggested, "Why don't you get him a wheelchair? Call the front desk and ask them for a wheelchair so he can participate in the last couple days of the cruise. It would be a bummer to be stuck in your room on a gala night when they undoubtedly will have a fantastic dinner. Maybe lobster again or at least prime rib. And remember, the final night's show will include staff who will serenade us with songs from their countries. It's fun."

"I didn't consider a wheelchair," I answered. "Great idea, thank you, Phyllis, I'll do it, but Griff is going to be madder than chickens in the rain. Quick question, ladies, are you wearing the same gown you wore at the last gala, or did you bring a second one?"

"I brought two, so I'll wear a different one," Carlee answered, "although the one I haven't worn shows off my turkey neck."

"Well, wash your neck, Carlee, for crying out loud. If you have a dirty neck, scrub it," Steve said crossly.

Phyllis laughed, "I only brought one dress, but I've miraculously lost a few pounds on this trip. If I can find one to show off my new dimensions, I'll buy it in a minute."

"I want to buy a second dress," Audrey announced, "Griff liked the red dress, but I'm becoming cruise crazy and want another."

"Your red dress was a heck of a dress," Gus sighed, "I vote for saving money and wearing the red one a second time."

"What's all this talk about an abscess? Who has an abscess?" Steve wanted to know.

# CHAPTER 79
### *Audrey*

Griff could have ordered breakfast through room service, but I delivered him a tray of waffles, piled high with fruit and whipped cream, bacon, orange juice, and coffee. I grabbed a couple yogurts and a donut on my way from the cafeteria and rode the elevator to our deck.

He was hungry and gladly took the tray, saying, "Wow, this is a great breakfast, Audrey. I've never had waffles with whipped cream. It's a real treat."

Griff had been elevating his foot and complained that the bunion splint helped but it was hard for him to walk because he thought he might topple over. I let him finish his breakfast and his complaining before I broached the subject of a wheelchair, "Griff, I'm going to request a wheelchair for you. You can't walk, and you're going to miss the last two days of the trip. Don't argue with me about it, I'm going to call the front desk right now. Otherwise, you will be confined to this room. I'd hate for you to be on house arrest on the last days of our cruise. We might rent a wheelchair in Lisbon, too, but let's see how your bunion progresses in the next couple of days."

Griff scowled and let me have it, "A wheelchair, you must be joking. What is the matter with you? I'm not crippled, I have a bunion. It's not going to happen."

I looked at Griff and he looked pathetic. I couldn't tell if he was in pain or reaching for sympathy. He was frequently irritable, but the bunion splint had moved him one more step up the crankiness ladder and I had

had enough. I was tired of being on the receiving end of his anger. He was surly, and I didn't want to be around him.

"Enough, Griff," I state emphatically. "That's true, you may not be permanently crippled, but your bunion and the bunion splint interfere with your walking, and I'm not going to sit here and coddle you and keep bringing you food. We have a gala night tonight, and I am going whether you do or not. I'd rather go with you, but you can't walk I'm done arguing." I phoned the front desk clerk and requested they deliver a wheelchair to our suite.

He was still grumbling and complaining, but I continued, "And now, I'm going to try to find a new dress to wear to tonight's gala. One of the shops had a beautiful black gown, and I want to see if it's still there. You'll be crazy about it because lets lots of skin show. I'll be back later and will show it to you," I told him matter-of-factly.

"That'll cost a lot of money, so what's wrong with the red one? If it's dirty, you could have it cleaned," Griff growled.

I responded, "No, it's not dirty, but people have seen it, and I want to look fresh."

"Hot is better than fresh any day, and you looked hot," Griff softened. "You heated me up in your red dress, and my magic wand is nearing an explosion remembering how you looked. Besides, we don't need to spend any more of our hard-earned soybean dollars."

I laughed, "Don't worry, Griff. We already spent our soybean dollars, but I still have hops dollars to plunder."

I exited the suite and took a deep breath. Logan was waiting, I hoped. I entered the Platinum Lounge where he sat sipping a latte. "I'm going shopping; do you want to come?" I invited.

The shops were full of people buying this or that. The last day of the cruise brought people out in force to fill their credit cards with purchases, flocking into the jewelry shops searching for bargains or the one special item to make their trip memorable. The staff had moved merchandise to the common areas where they hocked sweatshirts, hats, and other cruise wear to cram in a closet until their next trip. Reels of silver and gold chains allowed patrons to choose necklaces and bracelets at bargain prices.

Logan and I entered the shop where I had found the red and black gowns a few days earlier and noted the empty rack. "You didn't sell that gorgeous black gown you had last week, did you?" I asked, grimacing.

"Yes, we sold it just now. We marked it half price, and it sold immediately. I'm sorry, I don't believe we have any other dresses in your size, but I'll look again to be certain. Give me a second," the clerk said as he went into the rear of the shop.

"I'm disappointed, but Griff won't be. He liked the red dress and is worried we spent too much of our soybean and hops dollars," I told Logan.

"I agree that you spent too many soybeans and hops dollars on it, so let me spend my foot money. It would be my pleasure."

The clerk reentered with the same black dress I had loved in hand, "I was mistaken and found this one, identical to the one we sold a few minutes ago, but it was a different size. Do you want to try it on?"

I gulped in air at its elegance. "Perfect, it's simply perfect. I don't need to try it on, it'll fit fine."

"Well, I'd like to see it on you, especially if I'm paying for it," Logan insisted.

"You don't have to pay for it, Logan," I protested as the clerk wrapped up the dress.

"What would Griff say if I asked him about who should pay for it?"

Laughing, I said, "First he'd kill you, but then he'd say, okay, let the man spend his money."

"So, let the man spend his money," and he handed the clerk his key card.

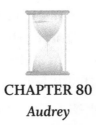

## CHAPTER 80
### *Audrey*

After buying the dress, I insisted on stopping at the ice cream shop. With fifty kinds of ice cream, hardly anyone could pass it by. Our time on the ship was coming to an end and this afternoon the chairs sat full of ice cream-eating patrons. Logan agreed, "I don't see any empty chairs, so how about we eat it in my cabin, and you can try on the dress. What if it doesn't fit or has a tear or is defective in another way?"

"I guess it would be okay, but no fooling around. Lemon sorbet, please. It's my favorite," I told the counter girl after scanning all fifty flavors.

"Cross my heart, no shenanigans," Logan assured me, then telling the counter girl, "I'll have the same, and could I also have a side of whipped cream and two cherries, please, and could we have lids?" Audrey eyed him suspiciously but didn't say anything.

When we arrived in his room, I said, "Let's eat this before it melts. Lemon sorbet is the best, it's so Italian. I haven't been to Italy, but I've read about it."

Logan shook his head, "No, not yet. Wait a second, sit down on the bed and close your eyes because I'm going to make you a sundae you'll never forget." He removed the dish from my hands and placed it on a nearby table before nudging me toward the bed and pulling the sandals from my feet. "Lie back and take deep breaths while I make your sundae." I lay back on the bed, dangling my feet over the side, and he sat on the floor with his feet stretched out in front of him and began his soda jerk

217

duties. He slid his fingers under and over my toes, across my arch, and over the heel, first one foot, then the other. "Deep breaths," he advised, "take deep breaths."

"I thought you wanted to make me a sundae?" I recalled.

"I'll make you into a sundae, just keep breathing," Logan answered.

I complied and closed my eyes. "Oh, wow, that feels good."

He breathed in and let his breath out slowly.

"Your beautiful feet give me goosebumps. He opened the container holding the whipped cream and began to daub dollops of whipped cream on my feet. "Your toes make me nutty," he moaned as he massaged the whipped cream in and around my toes, then kissed the sweetness off, while licking his lips. After each foot, he downed a Maraschino cherry, sighing with satisfaction. "You have the sexiest toes I've ever seen, they turn me on, make me crazy. I'm treating you to a toe sundae."

*What was this?* I had heard of a foot fetish but had never known anybody who had one. *A toe sundae? A podiatrist with a foot fetish? Who knew a podiatrist could be so sexy? He definitely knows feet.* I didn't say anything at first, but after a few moments, my body came alive with anticipation. My breasts swelled, my heart rate quickened, and my lower deck pulsated. I felt pleasure, real pleasure, unlike I had ever felt before. Not with Griff, not with anybody. "Oh, Logan," I whimpered, "Oh, yes, toe sundaes. Please, no one has ever kissed my toes before, and you are bringing my whole body alive. Don't stop. Please, don't stop." His hands were all over me, and I was primed for an erotic experience, but suddenly, out of the blue, my brain did a flip-flop, "Logan, stop. I can't do this. It's wrong, it's so wrong."

## CHAPTER 81
### *Audrey*

"Oh, Audrey. You are driving me crazy," Logan moaned, as he moved his hands northward, quickly reaching my breasts, moving to my face. He kissed me hard, and I kissed him back, simultaneously pulling away. I shifted away from him and in an instant, I was off the bed and spread eagle on the floor.

My body was on fire from my toes to my eyeballs, and my good sense had turned to oatmeal and I hurt in several places. I was frightened that I had come so close, too close, to succumbing to his seduction. He dropped to the floor and lay beside me, embracing me and pulling me toward him. "No, Logan, I can't." I repeated.

"Oh, Audrey, why? Why not?"

"Griff…" I said.

We lay quiet, Logan was frustrated, and I was frightened about what would come next, if anything. It was the kind of encounter I had read about, but never experienced. My body had calmed down, but I knew it wouldn't take much to reignite it. We hadn't needed pills or lotions, because our bodies manufactured everything we needed to satisfy both of us. We had nearly melted into one person, but yet…Griff. He was on my mind, front and center, and I couldn't ignore the fact that I was married. Married to Griff. I wanted Logan more than I had wanted anything, and it was clear he wanted me, too. We lay together on the floor for nearly an hour, neither of us moving, reticent in our own thoughts and fears.

Finally, we shifted and arose, but neither of our legs were working too well, and Logan cried out as he straightened his arthritic knee. My whole left side was numb. My mind was on Griff and what he would do if he knew what had nearly transpired, as in kill Logan. Or me. Or both of us.

Logan frowned, "Your ice cream has melted. We'll have to get more, but let's talk first."

"Talk? Yes, let's talk. I can't believe we came so close," I commented. "And the thing is, I liked it, well, more than liked, but I was still close to committing adultery."

"We came close, but not as close as I'd like. I love you, Audrey, I knew it from the moment we met. It seems like ages ago, but it was just last week, and despite your continuing rejection of my charms, I'm going to continue loving you. We only have a couple days before we get off the ship, unless, of course, we book another cruise and stay aboard," Logan suggested with a smile.

"That's a thought, but Griff..." I responded thoughtfully, as if it might really be an option.

"Yes, Griff," Logan agreed. "Do I have a chance in hell of being with you, Audrey? Or am I whistling warm air in a broken milk jug?"

I was astonished at myself. I hadn't sought this out, yet I hadn't fought it off either. And I was confused because I had been married to Griff for a long time, and it never occurred to me that I would betray him or that I didn't love him. But since retirement, he had traded romance for sex, while I, on the other hand, had become more interested in romance than sex, except now Logan might be changing all that. My newly over-sexed body told me he was interested in both romance and sex and maybe I was, too. I hoped so, but I still couldn't abandon Griff.

I wasn't sure whether my brain was working, so I held my breath, hoping for inspiration. None came, so I started talking, "This is the thing. Griff and I have been married a long time, but bit by bit the romance in our lives has vanished. He makes sure we play plenty of bedroom spin-the-bottle, but other than that, we don't have much in common anymore. Conversation about anything other than sex has atrophied badly and even a truckload of *salsa caliente* would be hard pressed to stop the shriveling.

Griff's life has revolved around farming and caring for our animals, and we did everything together before our boys left home, but when he retired, he began to focus on only three things: fishing, hunting, and sex."

"That sounds good to me, what's wrong with that?" Logan laughed, squeezing my hand. "I like them all, too!" Noticing that I wasn't laughing with him, he said, "I am glad we had this time, even though it wasn't how I wanted it to end. I do have a question for you though. Have you been honest with Griff about how you feel? I love you, Audrey, but I'm no homewrecker."

"In case you haven't noticed that rocket ship has already left Houston."

As I spoke, I became quite skeptical of my emotions toward both Griff and Logan. Logan appeared to want romance, and until an hour ago, had not mentioned sex, but that was an hour ago, and now things were different.

## CHAPTER 82
*Audrey*

Griff loved my new dress, especially since it had been half-price, but the backless and strapless style drove him wild. I hadn't told him that Logan paid for it. That little fact would be my secret. "Damn, Audrey, you look even hotter in this dress. You should dress like this every day, even at home. If it weren't for my bunion, we could do the dirty right now."

"Oh, yeah, I could wear it while I clean house," I laughed. "I love it, too, I feel like Audrey Hepburn, my namesake, when she played Eliza Doolittle in *My Fair Lady*, only she was about twenty, and I'm over three times that."

"You still have it, Kid, and I still want it," Griff drooled, grabbing me around the waist and tonguing me a kiss that I wanted to resist, but didn't. I had left Logan's room only an hour before, reeling over my encounter, if that's what I could call it. With Griff's kiss, I was even more confused. My brain and my heart stood at odds with each other, mixing rationality with guilt, and lust with pure joy. Logan was a soft down pillow and Griff was sandpaper. Everything he did or said grated on me.

I had specifically asked for a wheelchair, but while I was gone, the front desk delivered a three-wheeled knee-scooter. I called the front desk only to learn the wheelchair supply had been depleted, and the knee-scooter was the best they could do.

I helped Griff dress and read the directions for using the scooter: one leg pushed while the other leg rested on a seat-like cushion. Simple enough. I demonstrated how to use it and let him try it out. The formal shoes didn't fit over the bunion splint, so he wore one formal shoe and one black sock over the bunion splint. "I hate this, Audrey, I'm helpless."

"It's okay Griff, we'll never see these people again, so let's go meet our friends at the Night Sky Bar. It's my favorite watering hole, and tonight I plan to drink champagne. I want to celebrate this dream-come-true trip."

We slowly made our way to an elevator to carry us two flights up. Griff wobbled and bobbled at first, but finally balanced himself. Logan met us at the elevator door and helped Griff into a chair. He placed Griff's socked foot on a chair and made room for the other two couples.

"Now that's a dress, Audrey! The red one was sexy, but this one is starting fires. I am reconsidering my bachelor celibacy," Logan exclaimed.

Griff cast a disparaging look at Logan, and Logan was obviously stirred but couldn't unglue his eyes from me. He squirmed in his chair, "I think I need a drink. Scotch double, neat." Griff ordered the same along with a champagne cocktail for me.

We sipped our drinks and chatted and laughed while waiting for the others. Logan wore his new tuxedo with a black cummerbund and black tie, and Griff commented, "You're wearing a different tux, one resembling my junior prom tuxedo: a version of James Bond, shaken, not stirred."

"Bond drank martinis, and he seemed to be stirred by the women in the movies," I laughed. "I loved Sean Connery in the James Bond films; he was almost as sexy as the two of you."

Griff bristled a bit, but Logan chimed in, "We don't hold a candle to you, Audrey."

Steve and Carlee appeared, and Carlee stopped in her tracks, mouth open, not knowing what to do or say. I gasped, and my eyes grew to the size of Idaho potatoes. We wore identical dresses, the black strapless, backless gown. Carlee had purchased the other dress. We both wore pearls hanging loose around our necks, I had one strand, and Carlee wore two. "Uh, oh," we both declared simultaneously.

Logan moved his eyes from me to Carlee and back and said, "Isn't this interesting? Beautiful dresses on beautiful ladies."

Griff said, "What? What's wrong?"

"What do we do now? Shall I change into the red one?" I offered. "We shouldn't be wearing the same dress."

"No, you are right, this can't happen, and one of us has to switch gowns," Carlee answered.

"What's that about splitting gums? Is someone bleeding?" Steve asked, as he cupped his hand around his ear.

Carlee shushed Steve and we heard a robust laugh ring out from across the room where Phyllis stood. "Give me one good reason why we all shouldn't be wearing the same dress." We turned to see Phyllis clad in a black, strapless, backless gown, identical to ours. She moved toward us and linked arms with Carlee and me. She didn't wear pearls, but her charm bracelet tinkled.

Our whole table began howling with laughter, followed by the rest of the patrons. I said, "You know, why not? As I mentioned to Griff, we will never see any of these other people again."

## CHAPTER 83
### *Audrey*

Griff improved his knee scooter abilities, and we arrived at the dining room without incident. He enjoyed the attention he received moving through the passageways and dining room. Wheelchairs were commonplace, especially on a cruise of retired guests, but the knee scooter brought sympathetic looks, comments, and questions. Griff reveled at the attention.

The three of us identically dressed friends and our spouses, plus Logan, Mel, and, of course, Jack, spent our last gala night together, but it was bittersweet. Alcohol flowed freely, and we lamented that we had to leave the fun and frolic of ship-board life. We lamented the thought of returning to reality, and all of us fought back tears, even Griff. Family obligations and the drudge of life at home bounced through our minds. No more fancy meals. No more cabin stewards catering to our every whim. No more sea air. *No more sea sex on the balcony.* Logan suggested we all extend the cruise for another two weeks, which I thought was a dandy idea, but Griff put the kibosh on his idea, claiming poverty.

The cooks and dining staff paraded through the dining room to a robust round of applause for their tasty meals and service while guests stuffed gratuity envelopes into their hands.

The chore of packing loomed, and Griff and I decided to skip the show and return to our suite, but Logan invited us to the Platinum for one last farewell drink. Although more time alone with Logan was a priority with me, I asked, "Do you think we should have another drink? I had alcohol before dinner, wine at dinner, champagne, and now another drink. I've drunk more alcohol on this cruise than we've had in our entire lives. I've become a wine-a-holic and will probably go through withdrawals when we get home." In actuality, it was my toes and feet I was thinking about. Just thinking of Logan and his penchant for toes, stirred me.

"Don't be a fuddy-duddy, Audrey. It's okay because we can sober up when we get home. Logan invited us, and we don't want to be rude. We need to thank him for helping with my bunion. It is definitely on the mend, Hon," Griff assured me.

We visited with Logan for a while, and Griff drank a little more, "Logan's paying, so we might as well stock up," he suggested. "We should try to get the Platinum amenity with our next trip. It has to be less expensive than buying drinks by the glass." He remained unaware the Platinum had been our amenity, not Logan's, and I wasn't about to tell him.

"It's time to go," I pleaded, after imbibing a second glass of wine in near-record time, "I haven't packed, and it's almost time to put our suitcases out in the hall, so we need to get busy. Thank you, Logan, for inviting us. For everything." Logan took my hand and kissed me gently on the cheek. The kiss was longer than a peck and closer to my mouth than my eye, but who's measuring, anyway?

Griff didn't protest and picked up his freshened drink as he hopped one-legged toward the knee scooter. His hands grabbed at the handlebars, but the brake gave away and the scooter bolted as he attempted to clutch it. His teeter-tottering body crashed hard, coming down on his chest and his knee, twisting his torso and wrenching his back. Griff lay there grimacing in pain with one leg flung askew from his body, the other under the knee scooter, unable to stand. Logan didn't waste any time in calling the medical center, which was closed. The phone rang and rang before the reception clerk answered and paged Dr. Lewis and the EMTs to come to the Platinum Lounge. Moments later, Dr. Lewis and three EMT's arrived and hoisted Griff to a gurney and wheeled him to the medical center amid Griff's profane protests.

Logan and I followed the medical team to the clinic and after a series of X-rays, Dr. Lewis strapped leg and back braces on Griff and ordered him to be confined to a wheelchair, not knowing the wheelchair stock had been depleted.

"No wheelchairs are available, so, my friend, you will stay here with me tonight," Dr. Lewis declared emphatically. "I don't know what's with you men who think you are supermen, even though you can't stand or walk, let alone fly through the air."

Griff protested loudly, and I tried to calm him down, but he wouldn't listen. Finally, Logan stepped in and told him that he would not be able to get out of bed and use the bathroom if he stayed in their suite. Griff, still a little drunk, now had a bunion split, an injured knee, a wrenched back, and a very injured ego, but never fear, Dr. Lewis assured him, a wheelchair would be waiting when they disembarked in Lisbon.

Logan walked out of the clinic and waited for me near the elevator while I said good night to Griff. I covered him with a warm blanket, gave him a peck on the top of his head, and picked up his tuxedo, and shoe. "I'll bring a change of clothes when I come in the morning. I'll come early, to help you disembark. I can pack everything tonight, don't worry."

"Why did you bring Griff's clothes with you? He won't have any and I doubt he will want to get off the ship au naturel," Logan commented.

"Think ahead, Grasshopper…he can't get out of the clinic without clothes, and I hoped we could repeat our afternoon delight, but in my suite this time. I wouldn't want him to saddle his horse and walk in on us."

## CHAPTER 84
### *Gus and Phyllis*

When Gus retired at age sixty-five, he viewed retirement as the end of his life and told Phyllis, "I've done my thing, and I don't want to do anything else." From that day forward, he not only retired from teaching and coaching, he retired from life, except for a weekly round of golf with his coaching buddies. "I did my time, and now I'm done, finished, the same as when I left the Air Force. I'll relax, play a little golf, and drink a little beer, but I'm done with everything else."

On the other hand, Phyllis, retiring at age sixty-two, viewed her retirement from teaching and school activities as the beginning of her life. She told Gus, "We get to start over and do everything we've been saving time and money for: new and adventurous things. I have enough desires and energy for a trifecta of bucket lists." She immediately bought a charm bracelet to record her travels and began searching for cruises and other new and interesting things. Gus went along for the ride but didn't involve himself with excursions or other adventures. Just being on the ship was as much adventure as he wanted.

Five years later, they were still cruising, two to three trips a year, and Gus found the shipboard ambiance pleasant, although he didn't get excited about much, except the beer and the food. They had visited twenty countries, plus nearly every island in the Caribbean, except, of course, Cuba, since there weren't many opportunities to explore communist countries via cruises. She had disembarked at most ports alone, leaving Gus aboard the ship, but when she returned, he always waited for her at the security entrance, bringing smiles to the crew. "Mr. Gus is waiting for you inside the gate. He sure must love you, Miss Phyllis," they told her more than once. Of all the countries she had visited, she loved Italy the best, and of course, St. Thomas in the Virgin Islands, which entranced her with the most exquisite beaches. While in St. Thomas, she discovered fish pedicures that sexually aroused her, but she wondered at her sanity at being turned on by guppies. Nevertheless, she looked for fish pedicures at every port.

While Gus thought Phyllis' *new and adventurous things* only included cruises and visiting a plethora of cities and sites, she had other ideas. She found people more exciting than the excursions and discovered she especially relished personal encounters with men. Early on, she secretly set a goal to have sex in every country they visited, hopefully with a different man, especially since sex with Gus was mostly a no-show on most days. She had to concede that not all of her encounters were actually IN the country, but rather in port or on the way to a port. She filled her charm bracelet with her conquests, a silver charm for each. Gus thought she collected countries, but he was wrong. So far, she had only missed one country: Cambodia, excusable because she had managed two personal encounters in Thailand, and the Cambodian pickings were slim. She quickly learned Pol Pot's mid-1970s reign of terror still affected its current population.

She stocked up on various joy juices to maintain her libido, lotions, potions, and aroma therapy, plus several how-to books, which provided her with expertise and now her charm bracelet weighed her down.

Gus trusted her implicitly and while he drank beer and scanned the seas for dolphins and whales, she rediscovered sex as an invigorating activity, certainly new and adventurous. This trip had been successful because she had already nailed Griff and Steve, but not Logan, who probably was an easy mark, if she could get him alone without Audrey. She had never done a doctor. Well, Steve was a dentist, and that might have to do if she couldn't have Logan.

She loved Gus, and they had renewed their wedding vows the year before, but his romantic ambitions had waned with his age. He didn't like doctors, and when Phyllis suggested he see a doctor about the possibility of ED, he dismissed it. Between his weight and retired-from-life attitude, he had little interest in anything, including Phyllis. She knew she never had to worry about Gus having a fling with anybody. His desire for a new and adventurous love affair was located between zero and sub-zero. It was never going to happen.

# CHAPTER 85
## *Carlee*

Steve and Carlee and Phyllis and Gus stopped at the Rising Tide Lounge *for old time's sake*. The Safe Travels Special meant two for the price of one, so they ordered their favorites, wine for Carlee and Phyllis, gin and tonic for Steve, and a diet coke for Gus. "Doctor's orders," he complained. They had invited Dr. Lewis, but she was called to the clinic for a medical emergency.

Carlee gulped her glass of wine and smiled coyly at Gus, "Yes, we always do what the doctor tells us to do, right, Gus?"

"I don't want to leave this cruise," Phyllis whined. "It's been a blast, and I liked getting to know everybody. I added two charms to my charm bracelet, one for a sea voyage and one for Funchal. My bracelet is nearly full now, and I might have to buy a new bracelet for future cruises." She held up her wrist and jangled the charms.

"I'm ready to go home," Gus answered. "Spending time in the clinic is not my idea of a good time."

"Is that so? You seemed to be having fun both times I saw you there," Carlee said, "Dr. Lewis…well, she seems on top of things."

Gus shot daggered eyes at Carlee and would have thrown real daggers if any had been available.

"What do you mean?" Phyllis asked. "Dr. Lewis is nice enough, but she's not exactly my idea of fun. She's a few pounds overweight and should listen to her own advice about her size. It would help her out."

"She's oblivious to her weight because she has other things on her mind," Carlee retorted with a condescending look on her face.

"Like what?" Phyllis persisted. "What does she have on her mind?"

"Her patients, of course. She likes to get close up and personal with her patients. She likes to get to know them, I mean, really know them, right, Gus?" Carlee asked. "I've never seen a doctor so involved with her patients."

Steve couldn't hear everything she was saying but he heard enough and could tell by the look on her face that Carlee was in one of her snarky moods. He picked up his whiskey, saying, "We have to pack, Carlee, let's go to our cabin."

She stood up and snapped, "It's your turn to pack, Steve, and put the suitcases outside the door. I'm tired and want to go to bed. Put them out by eleven," she ordered. She picked up her second glass of Safe Travels Special wine and started back.

Steve shrugged his shoulders and clasped Carlee's arm who was having trouble with her balance, despite her grip on Steve's arm. She collapsed on the bed as soon as they entered the room, without undressing, still in her new gown.

Steve tossed out his whiskey and began to pack for the journey home. He didn't get angry easily, but Carlee raised his dander when he thought she was trying to implicate Gus in something that he was positive hadn't happened. She had done it before. He kept out a change of clothes for himself but packed everything of Carlee's into her bag and wheeled the suitcases into the hall, so the crew could take them to the dock for pickup tomorrow.

The next morning, Carlee groggily arose and looked for the suitcases, but they were gone. She had only what she had worn to dinner the night before, her black, backless, sleeveless, strapless gown.

"Oh, Steve, you didn't save any clothes for me to wear today. What will I wear?"

"I guess it's all or nothing," Steve said, smiling.

# CHAPTER 86
*Audrey*

Disembarking the cruise went well, although we had to wait for Carlee to find something suitable to wear. The three couples added extra time in Lisbon to tour a city none of them had ever seen. Logan had been to Lisbon before, but delayed his flight to spend a little more time with his new friends, including his FWB. His empty apartment in Fort Lauderdale would wait for him, unchanged and lonely, he justified.

While on board, the cruise line arranged for us to stay at the Lisboa Hotel Luxo, an older hotel near the pier with easy access to tours, including the trolley cars patrolling the city. The hotel had been modernized recently but retained many curious idiosyncrasies that the guests adored. It hosted three restaurants, three bars, and a generous outdoor patio serving both food and drink. Patio pigeons must have been welcome, as they perched on nearly every table scrounging morsels of food. No one shooed them away. All at once a blue bird with a yellow belly hopped from table to table. "Charlie Parker!" I called to the bird, but he only glared at Griff and flew away.

When we disembarked earlier, a wheelchair was waiting for Griff. Even though he said he was better and complained about having to use it, it was obvious that Griff needed the assistance. The three braces he wore on his body made that clear, but that didn't stop him from complaining even more when he was told the wheelchair had to be purchased and would be charged to his account.

Our group ate a late breakfast on the patio, discussing how to spend their one day in Lisbon before departing for home tomorrow on an early afternoon flight. Carlee, Phyllis, Logan, and I ordered fresh strawberries piled high in goblets with mint sprigs and fresh cream. Gus, not at his peak, opted for a cereal he had never heard of before. "I'll be glad to get back to my Cheerios and bananas," he told Phyllis when the server brought out a mashed-grain cereal mixture with syrup, raisins, and cream. Griff and Steve opted for eggs and bacon, and nobody chose the freshly made yogurt that didn't resemble anything American.

A trolley station was situated directly across the street from the hotel, allowing easy access to all kinds of city tours. We could see much of the city in only two hours. Immediately after breakfast, everyone except Griff caught a ride on an already crowded trolley car, number eighteen. Griff stayed on the patio and fed the pigeons. Charlie Parker reappeared and sat on the table, as if defying Griff and the passers-by. I headed toward the trolley first and quickly moved to the rear, tagging a bench seat and Logan followed. We all were surprised to see Dr. Lewis, who already was seated on the trolley.

She greeted us warmly, "It's good to see you. My contract with *The Broadwater* ended today, and I'm going back to the U.S. But, before I head back, I thought I would take another trolley tour of Lisbon. I've been here before, but I think the trolley ride tours are fun. Where are Griff and Gus?"

I answered, "Griff's feeding Charlie Parker, the ship's pet bird, and the local pigeons that are begging for food. Gus and Phyllis are on the trolley in the second row, behind Carlee and Steve. He's not well but is a good sport and came with us. This cruise exhausted him."

"I know he's not well," Dr. Lewis agreed, wrinkling her brow. "Maybe I should examine him to make sure he's okay for tomorrow's flight home. I'd feel horrible if something happened to him. I'm going to take Gus back to the hotel. Excuse me, please." She rose and squeezed herself down the aisle to where Gus and Phyllis were seated. Within moments, she had removed Gus from the trolley.

Phyllis followed them with her eyes and noticed Logan and me on the bench seat with one last space available and moved to sit with us. "Dr. Lewis insisted that Gus needs a treatment, I'm not sure what kind, but do you mind if I join you?" she asked while inserting herself between Logan and me.

Each rider had access to a set of headphones, and an English-speaking voice gave a non-stop commentary about the sites and history of Lisbon. Steve, of course, couldn't hear or understand what the speaker said, and after a few moments of turning unlabeled buttons and dials, he gave up and quietly watched the buildings parade by.

The multicolored tile buildings along the route fascinated us Americans; green, turquoise, burgundy, and bright yellow tiles with intricate designs bedecked every building. The trolley car hissed and rattled as it clattered its way through the tight streets where pedestrians had to place their backs to the wall and suck in their tummies while the trolley clanked by. Lisbon pedestrians applauded its strained efforts as it rumbled through the streets. Steve reached his hand out the window and snatched a leaf off a tree as it brushed the trolley and then raised it above his head in triumph.

The street widened, and more trolley tracks wound through the city, at times crossing each other, and both drivers would blow their whistles. Tiny shops and outdoor vendors offered items to the riders through the trolley windows. The trolley crept at a near snail's pace but even so, the riders had to be quick to view and pay for merchandise, but nevertheless, the vendors pursued.

Suddenly, the riders of trolley number eighteen heard a loud clank and a scraping noise as it brushed trolley number five, traveling in the opposite direction. Both trolleys thudded to a stop and the engineers jumped out in a flash. Soon, their hands became fists and fists became weapons and the dueling noses bled. Both trolley cars sat and waited and the riders in both trolleys didn't know whether to laugh or cheer or be horrified. Steve and Logan jumped out of their trolley to pull the two uniformed drivers apart. The drivers yelled in Portuguese that Steve could neither hear, nor understand.

Both drivers made phone calls and reassured their passengers that all was well before they returned to the trolleys and the impatient passengers who sat on the trolley tracks, waiting. It was all in the course of a day's work.

## CHAPTER 87
### *Audrey*

The six of us from Hunter plus Logan left for the airport early, planning to eat breakfast there, making a pleasant ending to a memorable trip. In his wheelchair, Griff barked orders and griped, but I warned, "Griff, for crying out loud, stop being Griff, and relax."

"I can't wait to get home," Steve whispered loudly to Carlee, "I hate not being able to hear. On the one hand, we've had a wonderful time. It was fun meeting and being a part of this group, and I hope we can remain friends when we return to Hunter. On the other hand, it has been hell because I can't hear and don't know what anybody is saying. It's been frustrating."

Carlee sympathized with him, "I get it, Steve, but try not to focus on your hearing and remember how you helped Mel and Jack. Jack might have died from an infection if you hadn't extracted his tooth. By the way, I haven't forgiven you for packing all my clothes and making me leave the ship in my evening gown."

"Are you kidding? You gave the crew a day to remember. You looked great. You should wear it around the house, you know, vacuuming and playing with the lawn goat. I wouldn't worry about my hearing if I saw you in that gown every day. By the way, how did you arrange first class for us? I thought we booked coach?" Steve asked as he reviewed their tickets showing them boarding in the first group.

"We did, but Mel called his travel agent and booked these seats for us. He was serious about paying you for helping Jack, but you refused, so he upgraded our tickets," Carlee explained.

Our travel agent, Cindy, also had booked first class tickets for our trip home. "Why the hell did Cindy book us in first class," Griff growled, "These tickets cost double those of coach, maybe more. And all you get is a cheese sandwich and a cheap glass of wine. Audrey, we need to spend less money. Your friend went crazy spending our money."

"Griff, relax. For starters, you can't walk and will need help getting to the bathroom. Your new wheelchair is with the cargo because it won't fit in the aisle. And, you know, Griff, we could have afforded to spend another lovely week in Lisbon. We did pretty well on the sale of our farm. But when we get home, I'll tell Cindy to be more frugal for our next trip," I agreed.

Gus was still ailing. Dr. Lewis had given him a prescription for Xanax to help him avoid another panic attack, but he felt sickly. He had lost twenty pounds since Dr. Lewis had started treating him, but he wasn't back to the old Gus. Phyllis requested they be bumped up to first class because of his ailing health, and the airline complied for a few dollars extra.

First-class was configured in rows of three seats allowing plenty of room to move about. Everyone had settled into their spots with an alcoholic drink, but three vacant seats sat empty in the first-class section. The flight attendant recognized Dr. Logan Hall was seated in coach and knew he had participated for many years in Doctors without Borders. She invited him to move from coach to first class, and he happily complied. He located Griff and me and immediately shifted me to the aisle, rationalizing that Griff might need help with his bunion splint and insisting that I might need more space. He claimed the seat between us and immediately offered Griff a sleeping pill he had in his medical bag. Griff, who couldn't stand to fly, and still in considerable pain, took it without hesitation.

As Gus and Phyllis settled in, a rotund woman appeared and told the flight attendant, "I'm Mr. Gustafson's personal physician, and I need to accompany him," Dr. Vivian Lewis exclaimed loudly and confidently. "He is not a well man and needs me. Excuse me, Ms. Phyllis, I need to sit by my patient." She shifted Phyllis to the aisle seat and sat between Phyllis and Gus, neither of whom protested.

Steve and Carlee were nursing their drinks when Mel and Jack appeared. "The flight attendant just bumped us to first class. The airline prefers service dogs to be seated in the front of the plane because the rear of the plane can get bumpy and may upset dogs. Not exactly a bummer for Jack and me. We're in first class, Jack. I hope they have tasty dog biscuits for you to munch on."

# CHAPTER 88
## *Couples*

The flight to Fort Lauderdale lasted several hours, and the dimmed lights presented an ideal opportunity for handholding, snuggling, and whispering. The flight attendants puzzled over the three couples and three singles, all of whom seemed to know each other in one way or another. They couldn't help noticing how easily these passengers switched their attention away from their spouses and onto, well, anyone. It was interesting, but they shrugged it off, having seen it all.

Logan held my hand throughout, and I rested my head on his shoulder. We both kept an eye out for Griff who slept soundly and Carlee who could be snarky. Griff had damaged both his back and his knee, and I knew he would be in pain when he awoke. And when he was in pain, he was such a baby.

Logan did not have another cruise planned for several months, giving him plenty of time to make sure everything was safe and sound in his home in Oregon. We talked some, and he told me he wanted to spend more time with me. I protested, knowing that would never fly with Griff, but Logan had devised a plan to offer his medical services until Griff had improved. He would come to Hunter, rent a car to drive to Portland, and I could ride with him to visit our grandchildren. Griff was always interested in saving money, especially after this trip, and I thought he might be amenable to this plan.

Midway through the flight, without saying anything more to me, Logan rose and went to the bathroom. But before returning to his seat, he stopped at the flight attendants' station and whispered, "I have a ticket to Fort Lauderdale, but I need to add a flight to Hunter, Idaho. I'm a physician and have an urgent situation. Can you add that leg for me, or will I need to change it at Lauderdale when we land and pass through customs?"

"I can do it, hang tight," the attendant answered, "but I'll need your credit card."

Gus, too, had drifted in and out of sleep, and Dr. Lewis was calmed as she listened to his gentle breathing. His hand fit her hand well and she wondered how she could have been so lucky to meet and treat him. Before long she rose to use the bathroom. She had been scheming, too. Before returning to her seat next to Gus, she also paused at the flight attendant's station, ducked her head so no one would hear, and made a request, "I need to extend my flight to Hunter, Idaho, but I am only booked to Lauderdale. I'm a physician with an urgent situation. Can you change my ticket here or do I need to exchange it when we land and go through customs?"

"I can do it, but I'll need your credit card," the attendant responded, puzzled.

When Dr. Lewis had gone out of hearing range, the flight attendant whispered to her colleagues, "Do any of you find it curious that both of the people wanting to change their tickets are asking to be re-routed to Hunter, Idaho? I guess it's true what they say about that place, a haven for swingers. And, clearly, geriatric swingers! It must be number one on people's bucket lists…"

## CHAPTER 89
### *Audrey*

It was the last hour before landing in Lauderdale and Griff was sleeping and everyone else was, too, when Logan nudged my arm and pointed to the bathroom. I looked up, thinking he wanted me to move so he could go to the bathroom, and adjusted myself so he could get by, but he had other things in mind and grabbed my arm as he passed me, pulling me along with him. The attendants were taking a break after a busy feeding time and first-class seating lay silent.

"The Mile-High Club," he whispered, "I've always wanted to, but never have. Are you game?"

"Are you kidding? We can't, I mean, Griff, and the others, they'd know. We can't do it," I mouthed back in protest while shaking my head. My mind was a rollercoaster, up, down, around, backward, and forward. What was I thinking?

"Everybody's asleep, it'll be quick, something you can write in your diary. No one will ever know, c'mon, Audrey, we'll never have another chance. Spontaneous, remember? Besides, I'm guessing they're gonna know sooner or later anyway, it might as well be sooner, if you ask me," he pleaded.

I had heard of the Mile-High Club but never really dreamed I might do it. I had refused Logan's advances the entire trip…maybe he would be satisfied with some deep toe-tingling kisses. Probably not, but he was right…spontaneity. I looked around and everyone was asleep, especially Griff, still affected by the sleeping pill Logan had supplied. No one else was stirring. The lights were out, except for emergency lighting, and the lavatory sat idle. "Let's go," he said again and ushered me in.

I took a second look at Griff, then Carlee, who appeared to be dead to the world, and whispered, "Okay, but quick, Logan. Really, really quick. Before anybody wakes up."

"I'm gonna redefine the word quickie because I am ready right now. Oh, Audrey, I'm crazy for you," he said, as we both entered the tiny bathroom, stumbling over each other.

I stepped on something and looked down. Phyllis' charm bracelet lay beneath my feet. She must have dropped it when she had used the facilities. I tried to reach it, but it was just out of my grasp. "Can you reach it," I hissed to Logan. He was taller and had longer arms, and I thought he might be able to stretch enough to pick it up, which he did. The two of us were wrangling for maneuvering space in the room with not much to spare, but suddenly the plane hit an air pocket and dropped, catching us unaware and we both pawed at each other. He still held the bracelet in his hand, while I seized his arm. The plane rocked one more time, and I banged against the door and he slammed his hips against the outer wall, where the flush button was located and WHOOSH! his foot and leg were instantly covered with an aqua liquid that sprang from the toilet. In an attempt to keep his balance, he automatically dropped the bracelet and watched as it flushed away into the most hidden of hinterlands.

The *return to your seats* light flashed on, followed by knock, knock, knock and an attendant saying, "Return to your seat, please."

I gazed at Logan, his green foot and leg, and found myself overcome by an overabundance of emotions. At that moment, all I could do was laugh. "No one will ever know, you said, but I kind of think they will. And what about Phyllis' charm bracelet?"

Logan also began to laugh, "I told you it would be something fun to add to your diary, and I have no doubt about that now."

When I opened the door, the lights shined bright and everyone except Griff, who was still out with the sedative, was stirring, trying to wake up but their eyes focused on me and Logan's green foot, and they all began to laugh.

Phyllis said, "Has anyone seen my charm bracelet? I had it right here."

I went to Phyllis and whispered in her ear, telling her about the toilet swallowing her bracelet, promising that Logan would buy her another.

Phyllis stared back at me and groaned, "Audrey, I had around twenty-five charms on that, and each one had such a special meaning." She paused, and I could tell she was mourning her loss. But then, something changed, and I could see a new sparkle in her eye, along with a sheepish smirk on her face, "I can start over…there are lots of adventures just waiting for me." Indeed, there were lots of adventures awaiting all of us.

# Acknowledgments

Thank you, Tom, for believing in me during our lives together, encouraging me by saying that I could do anything. We sailed the seas and reached all seven continents, although we did not traipse over the icebergs to touch ground in Antarctica, but saw three days' worth of ice, penguins, otters, and seals. I loved every minute of our cruise time. I'm missing you and love you. Always have, always will. Semper fi.

This series was given birth by my daughter Elizabeth and my editor Anna, who both told me to write a romance novel, but not being a romantic person, I laughed because I'm much too old for the bare-necked and bare-chested romance novels that lie on the library shelves. They told me I was thinking wrong, and that I needed to write what I know and to write a romance series for people over seventy. Since Tom had told me I could do anything, I said, *why not*, and they said *go for it*, and here they are. Wrinkly Bits.

Thank you to my editors, AnnaMarie McHargue and Anita Stephens, *Words With Sisters*, without your talent and time, I would still be floundering, as I continue to do most days.

Thank you, Linda Alden, for your tireless interest and assistance each time I got stuck. The four o'clock wine time helped, too.

Thank you to the many seniors who are involved in romantic hijinks, several of whom are my long-time friends. You gave me fodder for this series. I could name names but would not embarrass you for the world. Enjoy the journey!

Thank you to my Facebook followers for reading my bi-weekly blog, *Wrinkly Bits* or *Wrinklybits.com*. Writing can be a lonely process and receiving your comments and feedback encourages me and keeps me going.

Thank you to Elizabeth and Chris Hume and Cole and Pam Cushman for your continued support and for also giving me grandchildren to spoil. Nate, Tommy, Roe, Maggie: you brighten my day, every day!

I hope you enjoy my stories as much as I have writing them.

# About the Author

My husband often teased that I had two useless degrees, a B.S. and an M.A., both in Sociology, along with a quite a few classes in Psychology, but he was wrong. Those degrees made me a master of people-watching and now with twenty cruises and a lifetime of doing what I do best, I have observed more senior hijinks than I can possibly remember. I taught composition for eleven years and spent three years as a Marine Corps Officer. Retired, I spend my time writing, and currently author a bi-weekly blog "Wrinkly Bits" available at Wrinklybits.com. Age is only a number, get on with living.

CPSIA information can be obtained
at www.ICGtesting.com
Printed in the USA
JSHW040325020421
13171JS00003B/15